SPLINTERED

A True Story About Multiple Personalities

LuWanda M. Cheney

To Janet,

Thank you for your support?

LuWanda M. Cheney

BGB
Bronze Goose Books

THIRD EDITION

First edition published 2006, Second edition 2021, Third edition 2022

SPLINTERED is available in hardcopy, paperback, eBook, will soon be available in Audio, and can be purchased in quantities for educational purposes, book clubs, etc. For information contact BRONZE GOOSE BOOKS www.bronzegoosebooks.com

Author LuWanda M. Cheney is available for speaking engagements and book club discussions. Email info@bronzegoosebooks.com or call 508-304-1521.

Cover Image & Interior Designed by Danold

ISBN- 978-0-9788000-5-5

PRINTED IN THE UNITED STATES OF AMERICA.

In memory of
Angel
To me
she will always be
my little angel.

1942-2004

Acknowledgments

Writing a true story is a group effort. I thank my family and friends for their understanding while I was distracted and unavailable as I pieced fragmented memories together and put them in order.

I posthumously acknowledge Bony, Alberta, Betty, Gwendolyn, Ralph, and Edward for validating my memories, filling in missing pieces and providing locations.

Also, thank you to Carpe Stylum!- my writing group: Ed Orzechowski, Emily Bancroft, Tim Bancroft, Dr. Michael Finch, and Lisa Digris who supported me throughout this journey, and my designer, Danold Ampagoomian, without whose help I would not have been able to finish this book.

SPLINTERED

SPLINTERED

Author's Notes

Splintered is a true story. Someone, at some time, may come forward and say that this happened there, or that the dates are slightly off-kilter. But I have done my best to give a true accounting.

Some names and insignificant details have been changed. When I started writing *Splintered*, Angel asked if I was going to use real names. I told her some names would be changed for various reasons- to respect privacy, and to protect the innocent relatives of the guilty. She asked me to change hers because she never liked her own name much. In the book I call her Angel because when she was little, she looked like a little cherub. I thought it would please her. Sadly, she died before the book was finished. Now I call her Angel because it pleases me.

1

The first time I killed him he was somewhere in Idaho. The two-story house sat up on the rise, bathed in pale moonlight. There were no clouds in the ghastly white and desolate sky; the wind held its breath and the birds had gone and buried their song. Nothing, as far as the eye could see, except the house and a dead black tree that stood in front and off to the right. I started up the twisting path, which led me up the rise and past the mailbox on which someone had scrawled his name. Clayton Stout.

In the eerie white lightness of this silent place, I moved in slow motion up from the hollow. My bare feet scarcely touched the ground, as if I were floating. Slowly I climbed six steps onto a wide porch with a banister all around, the kind of porch I thought I might have some day, the kind where you expect to find wicker and ice-cold lemonade. I crossed the porch and stood before the door. On my left, a solitary chair, the colors on the cushion now faded the same drab gray as the burpled paint. A spider web hung suspended from the arm of the chair to the doorframe. A common housefly, caught in the delicate strands, struggled to free itself from certain death.

The door opened. Clayton Stout stood waiting. He was much smaller than I remembered. I expected someone more sinister. *He* seemed so ordinary. Checkered shirt, lumberjack boots, brown hair brushed back into a wave, nothing to distinguish his insipid face, except the eyes. I recognized those evil yellow eyes and the grinning, leering smirk.

He knew why I had come. His eyes widened and I saw myself reflected in them as I slowly raised my right arm, carefully placed the .357 Magnum against his left temple and pulled the trigger. The shot thundered, reverberating in my ears. I waited for him to die, my heart thumping against my ribs.

The next time I killed him I came up from the hollow in slow motion and climbed the steps onto the porch. It was all the same, except this time he sat motionless in the chair. He knew that I was no longer helpless, no longer innocent. I was Death. I towered over him, watching sweat ooze from every pore. One drop appeared upon his upper lip and dribbled down his chin. I calmly placed my perfectly manicured fingers around his throat and strangled him.

The third time I killed him he was an old man. He stood at the top of the steps, bent over and leaning on his cane. I stood at the foot of the steps, thinking he would be nicer dead.

Fierce wind whipped my hair about in a wild way. Then, as suddenly as it came, the wind ceased. Ominous thick mist came up from behind the rise, creeping around and over the house. I stood watching the fog swirl about my feet, and listening to a faraway mournful tone, the sound of a foghorn warning of danger.

Slowly I raised my arm- the one with the gun. At that same moment I knew he had tricked me. He leapt down off the porch, no longer a feeble old man. He had become the aberration I had known- a monstrous devil-man towering over me. His lips curled into a sinister grin. I could see those cruel, yellow eyes clearly. I pulled the trigger. The faint click, click echoed inside my head. He grabbed the gun and tossed it aside. It clattered to the ground. Busted. A toy. And I was, once again, a helpless child. He had a real gun, I knew, and a sharp knife.

Now he flung his cane at my feet. I watched, terrified, as it turned into a writhing serpent. The snake fixed its yellow eyes on me and slithered towards me. I turned to run and tripped and fell and the snake and I plunged headlong, whirling and spinning into a black bottomless pit.

I wanted Clayton Stout dead. Not for revenge. I had a much better reason than that. It was like that time the Grizzly went bad. It happened like this: A young homesteader hung a smoked ham on the stoop. The Grizzly smelled the ham and went after it. The man tried to chase him off with a broom. Grizzly smacked the man, knocking him down, and made off with the ham. The woman rushed to see if her man was all right. He wasn't. He sat, propped up against the cabin, hunkered over, his stomach yanked open by that grizzly claw and his guts sloshed out on the porch. While the woman was at the hospital finding out her husband was dead, the men in town formed a posse and went out and killed the bear. They didn't do it for revenge; they did it to keep the bear from ripping someone else's guts out. That's the way it was with Clayton and me.

When repressed memories surfaced, and I remembered what he had done, I dreamed up a thousand ways to kill him.

The memories came back in bits and pieces. When they surfaced, they returned not as memories but as a present terror, forcing me to relive the trauma. Strangely, as I fit the pieces together, my life became more scrambled. There was no way to escape the puzzle I had become. Like a jigsaw puzzle with pieces missing, I needed to piece myself together.

Clayton Stout had broken the child within me. My mind had splintered. A part of me had disappeared.

I rummaged through my mind, sifting through lost memories, searching for clues, and as each fragmented memory came to me like a flash of lightning in a black sky, I wrote them down in this book.

And I kept on remembering:

The first thing I remember is when I was three. It was the third week of June in '42. I was lying in a strange bed waiting for my daddy to come back. Daddy had dropped us off at a hotel in downtown Bremerton and gone to buy cigarettes. Mama was sitting by the window staring out into the night. Black. Except for the flashing "HOTEL" sign. Mama's big belly growled 'cause it was empty. She was hungry, same as me.

Mama was still sitting by the window when I woke up. The sun was up, the room already hot and stuffy. Mama's eyelids were swollen, her green eyes were leaking and her face was streaked with tears. Mama wiped her face with the back of her hand. "Good morning," she said. "Yeah, it's a real good morning. Nothin' to eat. Got one nickel to my name. But don't you worry. I'll get us out of this rat trap." She looked out the window one last time. "C'mon, let's go. He's not coming back."

Mama put her nickel in the pay phone in the lobby and called Grandpa, then we walked eight blocks to Western Union to get ten dollars. It was five more blocks to the bus station. Mama bought bus tickets. Coffee. Grilled cheese. Hot cheese scalded the roof of my mouth; blistered my tongue. I sucked in air, trying to put out the fire.

"Hey, take it easy," warned the blonde behind the counter. "Are you starving to death? Here, have some water. Anything else?"

I was hoping we could have apple pie, but Mama said, "Not today."

When Mama finished her coffee, we walked over to where the benches were, sat down and waited for the bus that would take us to Grandpa's house.

We sat pressed together in the hot bus while the sun cooked us. Mama stared out the window. Beads of sweat formed on her upper lip and ran down the left side of her droopy mouth. Mama's mouth got like that when she was tired. They tell me Mama had polio in '22. She was just a little bit of a thing with legs that didn't work. Twice a day, Grandpa lay Mama on the kitchen table and rubbed her legs with crushed herbs he gathered in the woods, then put her down on the floor and held out a peppermint. Mama cried pitifully, dragging herself across the floor. Grandmommy wanted to pick her up but Grandpa said, "No! Make her do it or she'll never walk." Every time she reached Grandpa, he moved away. "Come to Papa." When she could crawl no farther, Grandpa picked her up, cradled her in his lap and gave her the candy. Six months later, Grandpa walked eight miles into town, came back with a bag of candy and dumped it on the table. Mama crawled towards the table. Grandpa pulled her to her feet. "If you want candy you have to walk," he said. And she did. Eventually, the only sign of polio was a mouth that wouldn't behave.

Now Mama fanned herself with her bus ticket, wiped her crooked mouth with the back of her hand, then reached across me to open the window to get fresh air. It didn't help. The air outside was hot and steamy. Mama sighed. It's a long way from Bremerton to Grants Pass. It's a very long way to go in a hot bus.

————————————◆————————————

Grandpa met us at the corner bus stop. He smiled at me, and the corners of his eyes and mouth crinkled like nice old leather. He picked up Mama's suitcase in his strong, sun-tanned hands and headed for the house, Mama and me right behind him.

Grandpa's house was just past the hospital in Grants Pass, Oregon, on the opposite side of town from Rogue River. The big, old house sat in the shade of a walnut tree older than Grandpa and taller than the house. It was cool beneath the tree, and that was a blessing, hot as it was.

Grandmommy waited on the porch. She was a big, tall woman-not too big but not small either. Covered up proper, she wore a scarf round her neck, tucked into the neckline of her flowered dress and held in place with a cameo brooch, so as to hide her bosum. She threw her arms around my mama. Then she swooped me up and swung me round, telling Grandpa, "Oh, Albert, look at her."

"Betty Lou, y'all wash up. Supper's ready."

Mama's youngest sister carried me inside. "They call me Bones," she said, her voice deep and slow. "You can call me Aunt Bony." Aunt Bony was tall and lanky, even taller than Grandmommy. That's why they called her Bones, even though her real name was Marisla. Suntanned, with rusty knobby knees and elbows, she had brown hair and eyes, same as me. She was fifteen years old and could out-wrestle most boys. If you crossed her, she'd just as soon double up her fist and sock you.

Suddenly, the back door burst open with a bang and Uncle Ralph rushed in. Right behind him was Uncle Edward, which is not surprising because wherever you found one of the Vattell brothers you were likely to find another. Uncle Ralph patted Mama's big belly. "What you got there? A watermelon?"

Mama stuck out her lower lip and left it there until Uncle Edward told her she was beautiful. Mama grinned.

My uncles each grabbed one of my arms and carried me, swinging and giggling, to the supper table. Already I loved my uncles with their high cheekbones, black hair, and dark smiling eyes.

Mama looked over the table and nodded approvingly. "You still got the silver your mother gave you," she said, "and the Blue Willow china."

"Well, sure," Grandmommy said, like it never occurred to her to give it up.

I never saw such a table, or so much food. The delicious smell clobbered our noses. Before we could eat, we had to bow our heads while Grandmommy thanked Lord God Almighty for the food. Then she set a plate, piled high, in front of me. I gnawed on a chicken leg and attacked a mountain of mashed potatoes, stuffing my mouth and swallowing without chewing.

Grandmommy heaped food on Mama's plate. "Y'all must be hungry and plumb tired."

"Starved. Tuckered out."

Grandpa put down his fork. "Ralph is leaving tomorrow."

"Where are *you* going?" The way Mama asked, I could tell she'd rather talk about herself.

"I joined the Navy."

"Oh," Mama said in a quiet voice.

Now nobody talked. They paid attention to their plates, like the food was the most important thing in the world. They stayed quiet until supper was over, then Grandpa pushed his chair away from the table. "Ralph, let's get that whittling knife of mine you like so much. You can take it with you."

Uncle Edward jumped up. "I got some cherry wood for you to whittle."

After supper, Aunt Bony took me out back to the outhouse. Unlike most outhouses, this one had a window- a real one, with glass, and snow-white curtains, starched and ironed. On the shelf opposite the window was a half-gallon amber glass bottle of Clorox and a can of lye. With these two things, there was no smell. Aunt Bony pointed to an old Sears catalog that had been nailed to the wall. "After you go," she said, "tear off a page, crinkle it to make it soft, then wipe yourself."

She held me high above the dark hole. I went, then Aunt Bony put me up on her shoulders and carried me inside.

Grandpa rolled the little bed he had made for me out from under Aunt Bony's bed. It was feather-bedded and spread with one of Grandmommy's quilts. This one, shells pieced together from scraps of old silk party dresses. At the head of the bed lay a pillow fish with blue button eyes. Mouth embroidered red. Scalloped scales in pink, purple, blue, and a purple velvet tail.

I floated on a feathered sea, amongst the shells, clinging to my stuffed fish, with a full belly, the first in I don't know how long, and I was pretty sure we'd eat again the next day.

The door had been left open, just a little. In the light of the kerosene lamp, I could see Mama sitting at the kitchen table, hunched over the table, her big belly covered by her faded housecoat. Grandmommy reached for the blue-speckled kettle on the wood stove and poured coffee into Mama's cup. Mama added two spoonsful of sugar and lots of cream. Grandmommy looked at her over the top of her glasses. When Grandmommy looked at you with those clear gray eyes, you knew she could see right inside your heart. There was no use lying. Not to her. Nobody lied to Grandmommy. "Betty Lou, where's your husband?"

"Gone."

"Gone? Isn't he coming to be with you when the baby's born?"

"If he did show up here, which I doubt, I'd cut out his gizzard. My *husband*, if you can call him that, went to get cigarettes and left me waiting in a rat trap hotel. At first, I thought he had gone drinking, you know. I thought he'd be home any minute, then pass out like usual. But he never came back."

"Merciful Heaven." On the wall behind them, a Grandmommy shadow. The shadow's hand flew up to cover its mouth.

"He wasn't here when the first one was born, either." Mama said it way up in her nose in a squeaky, high voice. Grandmommy handed her a handkerchief and Mama blew her nose on the blue embroidered pansy in the corner.

"Lord God in heaven." Grandmommy poured more coffee.

"After two days, lying in that lumpy bed, I heard footsteps outside the door, then a key in the lock. I thought Merle had come back, you know, but it wasn't him. It was Bedbugs, the landlord. You don't have to guess why they called him that. He said, 'I seen your ole man ain't been around. You okay?' I told him, 'I am *not*. I need a doctor.' Bedbugs fetched the doctor, and seven hours later, at one minute past midnight, Doc handed me a squirming pink bundle. He said I was fine, then he told me Lucinda wasn't getting any milk."

I heard what Mama said. I was thinking, *Mama's telling the story about when I got born.*

"I looked down at that little bit of a thing with her big brown eyes staring up at me, her little mouth tugging at my empty titty, empty 'cause I hadn't eaten in two days, not a bite since I felt that first sharp cramp, you know. Bedbugs, bless his heart, brought me a plate piled up with fried potatoes and pinto beans. Then came back with milk for the baby."

"Praise the Lord. Thank you, Jesus." The Grand-shadow on the wall raised its hand straight up toward heaven like it was trying to grab hold sweet Jesus.

"I heated up the milk like Doc told me, and the baby drank the bottle, every last drop, farted and fell asleep. I laid her down on her full little belly, and you know where I put her? I took a drawer out of the chest and put a pillow in it. That was her *bassinet*." Mama wiped her eyes.

The shadow nodded like Mama had done right. "The Lord was with you."

Mama shook her head. "I *seriously* doubt it. Merle came busting through the door. I woke up and saw him at the same time I smelled him, reeking of whiskey- drunk as only a tough seadog Swede can be. He was a poor excuse for a sailor. He'd lost his hat. His shirt was ripped. He had a black eye. The baby woke up scared half to death by all the commotion, you know. She let out a howl, and that's when Merle finally noticed the baby. That sobered him up, all right. He fell on his knees, his arms around my waist, crying and begging forgiveness, promising promises he couldn't keep." In between sobs Mama said, "When I first met him he looked so fine in his uniform, standing tall, and smiling down at me, I thought if I married him I'd really be somebody, you know. But he turned out to be nothing but a plain ole drunk."

Mama handed Grandmommy the empty sugar bowl. "I need more sugar."

Grandmommy sighed. "That's it 'til we get our rations next month."

I leaned over so I could hear better and fell off the bed. Grandmommy saw that I was awake and knew I was getting an earful. "Little pitchers have big ears," she said, shutting the door.

My daddy loved booze. He loved Mama sometimes. Maybe he loved me.

Next morning, the sun crept under Aunt Bony's curtains and shone on my little quilt. I could see that I was in a fairy tale place with shells all around me, shells that glowed in the sun's early light and I could tell that they were magic.

Aunt Bony was awake, sitting up in her bed, sewing something red.

"Look, Aunt Bony," I whispered, "Magic shells."

"Magic shells?"

I pointed. "See? They're shining."

"Well, gee whiz, you little skunk, close your eyes and make three wishes."

I clung to the fish with the fanned purple tail, closed my eyes and wished out loud for a doll, a red wagon and a baby sister.

"Don't open your eyes!"

I kept my eyes shut tight and whispered my wishes over and over.

"Okay. You can look."

I opened my eyes. At the foot of my bed was a rag doll in a red dress. I ran to tell Mama. Aunt Bony followed me out the room, blinking one eye like she had magic dust in it. "It's magic!" I squealed, "The magic shells brung me a doll!"

But it seemed like nobody cared about magic.

Grandmommy put ham between thick slices of homemade bread, wrapped the sandwiches in brown paper and packed them in a cardboard box alongside an apple. Grandpa closed the box, wrapped string around it and tied it in a way that made a handle for carrying the lunch.

Uncle Ralph came into the kitchen, Uncle Edward tagging along after him, a duffel bag thrown over his shoulder. Grandmommy motioned to the table. Uncle Ralph sat down and ate scrambled eggs.

Biscuits with thick milk gravy. A piece of ham, too, brought over by a neighbor. "For your boy, before he goes," he said.

Uncle Ralph took a bite, closing his eyes like he was committing it to memory. "Umm," he said every now and then.

Grandpa sharpened the whittling knife one more time, put it between a folded piece of cardboard, tied a string around it and tucked the safe-wrapped knife in the duffel bag. Uncle Edward stuffed the whittling wood into the duffel bag, then Grandpa tied, untied, and retied the duffel bag until it was shut just right.

Grandpa's house was on the corner. The bus stopped there, just past the rose bush. While we waited for the bus, Aunt Bony stood, staring at her bare feet for a long time, then reached into her back pocket and pulled out her lucky rabbit's foot and handed it to Uncle Ralph. She didn't say anything and neither did Uncle Ralph.

Mama's mouth was acting funny. She couldn't make it do what she wanted. She bit her lip. When she thought she had it under control, she said, "Take care of yourself, Brother." She slipped him an envelope. In it, the family's last five dollars, four postage stamps and a comic strip of *Beetle Bailey* Aunt Bony had cut out of the newspaper.

Grandmommy handed over the cardboard lunch box. "I made you a ham sandwich for the trip, so you won't go hungry."

When she said that, Uncle Ralph put his hands on his hips and danced a jig across the lawn, singing 'bout some sailor man.

Aunt Bony was grinning. Uncle Ralph kept on dancing and singing, his face flushed, wavy black hair rumpled, black eyes sparkling, until we were all laughing hard. When you got the Vattells tickled, they laughed honest open-mouthed laughs originating in the belly, not trying to be refined or anything like that.

The bus came too soon. Uncle Ralph took a deep breath, then let out the air. "Well, I guess this is it." Grandmommy handed over the cardboard lunch box. Grandpa put the duffel bag in the belly of the bus. Uncle Ralph stepped onto the bus, turned, and waved goodbye. "I'll be back," he called out as the bus swallowed him up.

Grandmommy headed straight for the rose bush, got down on her knees and attacked it with the scissors she kept in her apron pocket. She cut off every little part that didn't suit her fancy, all the while arguing with Jesus about the war.

Aunt Bony swallowed hard. "Gee whiz, Betty, will we ever see Ralph again?" When she said that, Uncle Edward took off, riding his bicycle down the road after the bus. Grandpa brushed his arm across his face and wiped away the tears.

"Mama?" I said.

Mama said, "Shhh."

––––––––––•••••––••••••––––––––––

We were poor, like most everybody else during the war. We were clean, hard-working and well respected. Nobody ever called us white trash. It's true- the house was dilapidated. Grandpa had bought it for the corner lot, planning to build a new house there. When the war started, he had to wait. It's also true that the kitchen cupboards were just orange crates nailed to the wall. Grandpa sanded and varnished them, and Grandmommy tacked red gingham curtains across the openings.

We didn't feel poor. We had plenty to eat. Grandpa had a garden and fruit trees. Apples. Peaches. Cherries. Walnuts. Grandmommy canned all summer, putting up 300 jars for winter. While she canned, she prayed, "Lord, watch over my boys gone off to war. In the name of Jesus. Amen."

Even though meat was hard to come by with the war and all, we didn't go without. Grandpa raised rabbits, the hutches lined up in a row like the government houses Mama said we were *not* going to live in. I remember Grandpa reaching into one of the boxes and cradling a naked baby rabbit in his hand. God hadn't given it a fur coat yet. Its eyes were shut tight and the small pink ears lay flat against its little head. I ran my fingers gently down the pink body and felt the tiny heartbeat, then Grandpa put it back with the mama rabbit where it belonged.

Grandmommy had chickens and an ornery cuss of a rooster almost as big as me. The rooster liked to stretch out, make hisself tall, then run at you, flapping his wings. It was enough to scare you half out of your wits. We were there just a few days when the rooster jumped on me, beating me with his wings and trying to peck at my eyes. Uncle Edward came running, waving his arms, circling like a hawk, and hissing, "Shoo! Shoo!" The rooster wouldn't quit. Uncle Edward swooped down and grabbed the rooster's feet. The rooster, held at arm's length, upside down, dangled helplessly. Uncle Edward threw him in the hen house and slammed the door.

Grandmommy saw the whole thing from the kitchen window. She pressed her lips together and stomped off towards the shed. "Hold the door shut," she said, as she slipped inside. Soon we heard a terrible ruckus. Hens clucking. Rooster squawking. Grandmommy yelling, "I see you, you black-hearted old cuss. Try and peck my granddaughter's eyes out, will you? That's the last thing you'll ever do." The commotion got worse. Pieces of firewood went flying and crashed against the wall. Then we heard a terrible loud squawk and Grandmommy emerged with the rooster in one hand and an axe in the other. She had the rooster by the neck, swinging it round over her head.

"What you doing, Grandmommy?"

"Wringing its neck." She put that ornery rooster on the block and chopped off his head! The head was dead. Dead eyes staring. The rooster wasn't. He was running round and round with his head cut off, blood spurting and splattering, bloody body chasing me. Grandpa swooped me up and carried me inside.

I was grinning like a fool. I knew now that nothing bad was ever going happen to me.

2

Before I ceased to exist, much had happened: It was 1942. Everybody was talking about World War II. Not yet three years old, I had no idea what they were talking about. Unable to comprehend the hardship that was all around me, and surrounded by love, my life at Grandpa's was magical. By now, the whole family understood that the quilt Grandmommy had given me was magic. The shimmering silk shells had already granted my first wish- a rag doll. Now, Grandpa took my hand and led me out the back door and across the dirt road to a big ole shed that was his workshop. "Those magic shells told me to make you something," he said.

Grandpa's workbench was long as two broom handles laid end to end, the color of chewing tobacco and crisscrossed with saw cuts. Along the wall, at the back of the workbench, were jars of paint, all colors, and nails of every size. I breathed in the fine smell of a carpenter's workplace. Sawdust. Turpentine. Linseed oil. I sat on the tall wooden stool with my elbows on Grandpa's workbench, my chin in my hands, watching Grandpa. His eyebrows were bushy. Black whisker bristles grew out his chin. He was over fifty, yet not one bit old. His hair was still black, and he walked straight and strong, not like some folk- the ones that have one foot in the grave the day they turn forty.

Grandpa rummaged through a wooden box of scrap metal until he found a sardine can. With pliers he pinched all around the rim of the can until the sharp edge was smoothed down. He turned the can on end, and, with an ice pick and one tap of the hammer, poked a hole clean through. Grandpa's rough, brown hands shaped stiff wire into a handle and an axle for washer wheels. He painted my little wagon red, just like I told the magic shells. My second wish had been granted. I could hardly wait for the magic shells to grant my third wish- a baby sister.

I was pulling my little red wagon across the kitchen table when Mama hollered for me to bring her a towel. I jumped up, glad to have Mama calling me. Generally, she didn't have much use for me. Mama was in the bathroom. Naked. I saw a black hairy thing hiding down below her big belly. I pointed. "Uh oh, you got a bogeyman," I said.

"It's not a bogey. It's my pussy."

"Can I pet it?"

"No."

Mama stared, wide eyed, at the puddle on the floor. "Tell Grandmommy my water broke." I wondered why Mama would pee on the floor and then fib about it but before I could ask, Mama screamed. Grandmommy came running and shooed me away. "Hon, it's breech," she shouted. Grandpa sent Uncle Eddie next door to the hospital to get help. "Tell 'em I'll fix whatever they need done."

Uncle Eddie came back with a nurse. "Aunt Bony," I said, "They brung a table with wheels." Grandpa carried Mama outside and put her on the table. Uncle Eddie and the nurse wheeled Mama over to the hospital where a doctor waited at the back door. All the while, Mama was screaming something awful.

A few days later, Mama came home with my baby sister. That's how I got my third wish. Now I had a rag doll, a little red wagon and a baby sister, just like I told the magic quilt.

Mama's big belly was gone and so was the bushy pussy that had been there before she went to the hospital. "Where's your pussy?"

"They shaved it."

"I feel sorry for that pussy."

Mama grinned. "Oh, I'll get another one *almost* as good."

Mama named my baby sister Gwendolyn Merle. She lay in the cradle Grandpa built, wrapped snugly in pink flannel. She was asleep, making sucking motions with her tiny mouth. Aunt Bony said, "Gee whiz, Betty, look at her. She's dreaming about sucking on your titty. Why don't you let her?"

"I don't want some baby gnawing on my titties, stretching them out so they'll sag afterwards, you know."

Aunt Bony shuffled her bare feet. "Gee whiz, I can't wait to get some babies of my own. I'm gonna let 'em chew on me all they want. Do you wish you didn't have kids?"

Mama didn't answer.

I stood over the cradle, watching my baby sister sleep. Mostly that's all she did. When she was hungry, she'd scrunch up her face and let out a howl, and sometimes, like now, she wrinkled up her face and dirtied her diaper. Mama sighed and handed her to Grandmommy. "Mama, what am I gonna do with *two* babies and my husband gone?"

———◄———————►———

It was July and hotter than the devil's kitchen but that didn't stop Grandpa. Every day he put on his double-breasted wool suit, white shirt, tie and a hat, and trudged across town in the sweltering heat to the carpenters union hall, the stiff white collar chafing his neck, then shuffled slowly home, drenched in sweat, to report, "No work today, Hon."

"You'll find something soon. Knock on wood." Grandmommy knocked on the table.

Grandpa shook his head, "Even with all the young men gone off to war, work is hard to come by. *Women* got all the jobs. I saw one driving a bus. Wearing *pants,* too!"

"Dear Jesus, what's this world coming to?"

"Papa," Uncle Edward said, "we can get relief if you can't get a job."

Grandpa frowned and rapped Uncle Edward up top his head, rolling his fist so that each knuckle clunked in turn. "We don't believe in relief. A man takes care of his own family. We don't do what's easy. We do what's right, even if it's hard."

And it was hard– all of it.

"The Lord will provide," Grandmommy said.

Grandpa sighed. "The Lord helps those who help themselves. We can help ourselves by picking hops."

Next morning, we got up early, dressed in the dark and crept downstairs to the kitchen where Grandpa had the kerosene lantern lit. Surprised to see Mama and me up and ready to go, Grandpa scrunched up his forehead. "Betty, you stay home with the babies," he said through clenched teeth.

"Papa, I need money, you know."

"You don't need money here. You stay home."

"But Papa—" Mama started.

Grandmommy interrupted. "Betty Lou, you cannot bring that baby to the hop fields. She'll burn to a crisp."

Uncle Edward saw Mama's lower lip quivering. "Betty, you can have my money," he promised. "I'll give you whatever I make."

Mama stuck out her chin. "I want my *own* money. Missus O'Reilly could watch the baby."

"Well," Grandmommy said, "go ask."

It's hot picking hops. There's no shade. You wear long sleeves, or you get sunburnt. You wear straw hats, or you get sunstroke. All day long the sun beat down on us. The hop vines wind themselves up strings tied to wires- one up high, and one down low, nearly to the ground. To strip them off the vine you have to reach up high, then bend low. Up. Down. Up. Down. Our backs ached. We got dirt on our faces, dust in our mouths. We worked shoulder to shoulder, stopping only occasionally to drink water.

Mama straightened up and rubbed her back.

"You tired, Betty Lou?" Grandmommy asked.

"Not yet. You?"

"I'm fine. You kids rest when you want."

"We're not tired. Papa, you tired?"

"Nope. Glad for the work," Grandpa wiped sweat from his forehead.

Uncle Edward nodded in agreement.

Aunt Bony said, "Well, shoot, we're lucky to have jobs."

Mama rolled her eyes. "Yeah, sure are *lucky* to get a job picking hops."

Grandmommy poured water on her handkerchief and wiped her face, now bright red from sun poisoning. "The Lord does provide," she said. "Thank you, Jesus."

"What time is it?" Mama asked.

Grandpa looked up at the sun. "Long about noon."

Mama sighed. "Is that all?"

When the noon whistle blew, we stopped working. Grandpa counted our full gunny sacks. "That's a fine morning's work," he said proudly.

Grandmommy motioned to a water pump at the edge of the field. "Y'all wash up," she said. Originally from Texas, Grandmommy still sounded like a Texan.

We ate sitting on the ground. In Grandmommy's basket were fried egg sandwiches on thick sliced homemade bread, a gallon jar of lukewarm peach juice and a jug of coffee.

After lunch the gunnysacks took longer to fill. Even Grandpa stopped to rest now and then. Mama worked right alongside the rest of them but stopped to rub her back every few minutes, all the while going on about hard times, the war, and how she was tired of working like a dog. "Bones," she whispered, "I've got to get the hell out of here. You know."

"Gee whiz, Betty, where would you go?"

"Anywhere but here. You'll see. Someday, I'm gonna be somebody, you know. And I sure as hell won't be pickin' hops."

At 6 o'clock, twelve hours after the hop picking started, the whistle blew. We traded full gunny sacks for money, then climbed up in the back of the big green truck that transported workers to and from the field, and headed home. We did the same the next day. And the next.

By the fifth of October, the hops were gone. So were our jobs.

––––––––––––––––––––––––––

Mama sat staring across the room at the piano. After a long time, she got up, walked across the room, sat down at the piano, played something I never heard before and began singing a sad song. Grandpa grabbed his fiddle and made it cry. Mama stopped playing abruptly. "Papa, if I leave this town, I can get a job playing piano."

Grandpa's forehead wrinkled. "You got no business gallivanting."

"But Papa, I want to make something out of myself!"

"Your place is with your little girls." Grandpa put down the fiddle and stomped away.

"Husband gone. Two kids. No job. What else can go wrong?" Mama said, under her breath.

––––––––––––––––––––––––––

Uncle Roy's wife, Ethel, screamed and a baby popped out. "It's a boy." "Blue." "Stillborn," they said, and shook their heads. "Ain't it a shame?"

"Where's Roy Junior?"

"Edward took him out to feed the rabbits. "

Uncle Roy built a small pine box for the baby. He sanded the box so hard and for so long that the tips of his fingers bled. Grandmommy said, "Roy! Roy!" He didn't hear. She put her hand on his shoulder. He didn't even notice.

Grandpa got the finest sandpaper he could find, handed a piece to Uncle Roy and stood beside his son. They sanded the box together. Finally, Grandpa said, "It's finished. It's a fine job." He took the sandpaper from Uncle Roy and wiped his bloody hands.

Aunt Bony whispered, "There's blood on the coffin."

Grandpa wiped the little box with a rag soaked in turpentine, then rubbed it with linseed oil. Grandmommy wrapped the still, blue baby in a blanket and put him in the box. Grandpa nailed the box shut, using tiny nails, and tapping gently. Uncle Roy laid his head on the box and wrapped his arms around it.

It was mid-afternoon when we got to the church. Instead of going inside, like usual, we trudged out back to the grassy church yard where a black crow sat, perched on a wooden cross. "Let the children come to me, for to such belongs the kingdom of heaven," the preacher said.

Church ladies dabbed at their eyes. Men looked at their feet. Choir sang. Ethel sobbed in Grandmommy's arms. Little Roy hid his face in Uncle Edward's chest.

The preacher tried to wrestle the tiny coffin from Uncle Roy. He wouldn't let go. Grandpa said, "It's time. Let him go." Uncle Roy handed over the box.

Brother MacDonald laid the little box gently in a hole in the ground.

"Ashes to ashes," he said. "Dust to dust." Then he picked up a shovel and scattered dirt on it. When he did that, Uncle Roy ran at the preacher, swinging with both fists. Grandpa managed to pull him away, but not before he gave the preacher a black eye.

"He's not right in the head," Mama whispered to those close enough to hear, "He was helping to put a new roof on the church, you know, and he fell off and landed on his head. He hasn't been right since. And now losing the baby. He's not right."

Brother MacDonald heard Mama. "No need to make excuses," he said. "We all feel his pain. No man ought to have to bear the sorrow of losing a child. There is no blame."

I didn't blame him one bit. And I sure didn't want to get put in some hole in the ground and get dirt on top of me.

Ethel lay in a dark room staring at the ceiling. Aunt Bony blinked hard. "Gee whiz, it's been almost a month. Has she gone plumb crazy?"

Grandmommy said, "Hush your mouth."

"But what's wrong with her?"

"Broken heart. Migraine. She'll come around in time."

Roy Junior sat on the floor next to the bed. "Mommy?" Ethel paid him no mind.

Grandmommy said, "Roy, let me take him. We can keep him till Ethel gets better."

"No. You've got too many mouths to feed as it is."

Another week went by. Ethel was no better. Uncle Roy said, "Ethel, the baby is gone but Roy Junior is still here. He's only five. He needs his mother." Ethel didn't answer, not even when Uncle Roy told her, "If you won't take care of our boy, I'll have to find someone who can." That same day, Uncle Roy took Roy Junior by the hand and trudged all the way across town, stopping at Piggly Wiggly to buy his son a candy bar.[1] Half an hour later, they came to a large brick building and went inside. Uncle Roy came out alone, his face wet. He threw a kiss at the barricaded door, somewhat comforted, knowing that rich folks brought food to the orphanage so the children wouldn't go hungry.

---

1. During the war chocolate and sugar were rationed. A 5¢ candy bar was a special treat.

Then he took off, walking fast, and joined the Navy— not to serve his country, like his brothers, but so Ethel would get $20 a week from Uncle Sam.

Grandmommy trudged down to the orphanage and pleaded with the officials to let her have Roy Junior, but they wouldn't let him go. Now she prayed for Ethel's migraines, Roy Junior, her own three boys gone off to war, and the daughter with two baby girls and a gallivanting husband.

———————◆————◆————◆———————

There was a chill in the air. The leaves on the walnut tree turned yellow and fluttered to the ground. Walnuts dropped with a thud. Grandpa and Uncle Edward cracked the nuts, Aunt Bony and Mama chopped them up and Grandmomy made cookies to send to the war.

Towards the end of the month, it rained five days straight and Mama was stuck in the house with a fussy five-month-old baby. As soon as the rain stopped, Mama took to sitting on the stoop, smoking cigarettes, and staring at nothing. Grandmommy brought her a cup of coffee. "Betty Lou, I can't help but notice that you've got that stubborn look on your face. Determined, like a fledgling gets when it's getting ready to leave the nest."

"Winter's coming, you know. There's no jobs here. I've got to get away from here."

"Don't you be thinking about flyin' the coop. You might get your tail feathers caught in a cross wind."

"I got to go someplace, you know, where I can make something outta myself."

In November, when Grandpa went off to look for work in the next county, Mama saw that as an opportunity. As soon as Grandpa left, she hightailed it into town.

Grandmommy climbed up on the kitchen table and swept cobwebs off the ceiling. I heard her say sternly, "Lord, I want you to end this war. In the name of Jesus, keep this family together."

I sat on the steps hugging my rag doll, thinking maybe Mama had gone to get cigarettes like my daddy and wasn't coming back. Aunt Bony perched up on the porch railing and kept an eye out for Mama. "Betty has something up her sleeve," she said. "I wonder what she's up to."

Mama came back from downtown with a package under her arm, went straight to the bathroom, locked the door, and stayed in there two hours. She came out with a Toni home perm, painted lips and wearing a new dress. Red. She was carrying a suitcase.

Aunt Bony blushed. "Well, Betty, you've got the body for it."

You'd never have guessed Mama had two kids. She wouldn't have told you either. "Betty's a good-looking woman," they said. "Maybe not as good looking as *she* thinks but her face ain't half bad, especially those green eyes. And she's built like a pin-up girl."

"Gee whiz, Betty, where you going?" Aunt Bony reached out to touch Mama's curls.

"Away from here. Brothers gone. Fighting *war*. Dead babies. Kids in orphanages. No money. I can't take it anymore, you know. I got to get out. I'm gonna make something out of myself."

Then Mama picked up her suitcase, and without a word to me, walked to the corner and climbed aboard a Greyhound headed for Las Vegas.

3

“**D**on't you be cryin' now, you hear?” Grandmommy said when she saw my puckered chin. “Come help make bread.” I wiped my tears when Grandmommy handed me an apron the color of the sun, with a green sash and a brilliant bird embroidered on the pocket. Aunt Bony wrapped the sash around my waist twice and tied it in a bow in the back The apron hem grazed the floor. I felt like a fairy princess in such a fancy apron. and I wondered why Mama didn't want me.

I climbed up on a chair and watched Grandmommy stir yeast into warm water. I sniffed the good smelling yeast, watched it foam and fed it a little sugar. Then Grandmommy added butter to scalded milk and mixed it with lots of flour and a little salt. She divided the dough into seven loaves, covered it with a towel and set it on the porch where the sun could warm it.

When the dough swelled up twice its size, Grandmommy clobbered it. “*That's* 'cause my daughter-girl is gone,” she said, punching the dough. “*That's* 'cause my boys have gone to war. *That's* 'cause I'm too old to look after these little girls. And *that's* 'cause I'm disappointed in *you*, Lord." By the time she was through punching the bread, her cheeks had turned pink and there was sweat on her forehead.

I stuck my fists into my dough and socked it again and again. "*That's* 'cause my mama's gone. *That's* 'cause my daddy's gone. And *that's* 'cause I'm *mad*!"

Margaret O'Reilly, the widow across the street, smelled fresh baked bread and knocked on the door. "My, my, something smells mighty good, Mae." Missus O'Reilly was small and thin like a stray cat. Her sparse, wild hair had managed to escape from the bun on top her head and stuck out in all directions. Her dress was wrinkled. Her shoes didn't match, and the brown shoe had a mite higher heel, causing her to waddle from side to side.

"Can I trouble you for a cup of tea, Mae," she said, talking fast, without taking a breath. "And to read my fortune? Look at all that lovely bread. I used to bake when Mister O'Reilly was still breathing, God bless his soul, and before Frankie went to war. Not anymore. When Frankie comes home, I'll bake a pie, that's what I'll do, I'll bake a cherry pie. He'll like that."

Grandmommy put the speckled kettle on. "Won't you stay for supper?"

"Don't mind if I do."

We ate the bread hot, with lots of melting butter, dipping it into steaming bowls of split pea soup. "That's good soup, Mae. Can I trouble you for another cup of tea and a wee bit more butter?" Missus O'Reilly licked her fingers. "Where'd you say you got all that butter?"

"Roy's wife, Ethel, has a cow."

"You don't say? That's good butter."

"We have plenty, knock on wood. You're welcome to take some." Grandpa said, "Take some milk, too."

"The Lord bless and keep you. And what'll the tea leaves be telling you today?"

Grandmommy studied the bottom of Missus O'Reilly's cup. "I see someone at your door," she started. But before Grandmommy could finish telling her fortune, Missus O'Reilly jumped up. "Oh, it's Frankie. It's my Frankie come home. I'll be going now. I'll be needing to get ready for Frankie. You be a good boy, Edward. Marisla, you help with the little ones, their own mother gone, God only knows where. Bless you, Mae. Evening, Albert."

Now three of my uncles had gone off to war. Uncle Edward said he wanted to go, too, but Uncle Sam said he was too young 'cause he was only thirteen.

I didn't know what they did at the war but whatever it was, it made everybody sad. It made them cry is what it did.

Every night we gathered round the radio and listened to Walter Cronkite talk about the war, 'cause he was the most trusted man in America. When he was done talking about the war, he would say, "And that's the way it is." Then Grandmommy would fall to her knees and beg Lord God Almighty to end the war and bring her boys home safe. Sometimes, Grandpa would get so mad at Walter Cronkite for talking about bombs that he didn't even listen to The Lone Ranger to find out what he and Tonto were up to.

Grandmommy sent cookies to the war and thanked Sweet Jesus and Lord God Almighty that she got letters, instead of a telegram- on account of that's how bad news traveled. Every day, she waited at the mailbox for the mailman to bring letters. Most days the mailman would shake his head and say, "No mail today, Mae."

Once a week, a letter came from Mama, and there was always a check in it. Grandmommy would hold up the check for Grandpa to see. "Betty Lou sure isn't stingy," she would say. Then we would walk cross town to Piggy Wiggly and get flour, corn meal, rice, beans, and sugar -if they had any. Sometimes, we got molasses so Grandmommy could make cookies.

On the days a letter from the war did come, Grandmommy held it up over her head and waved it in the air. Aunt Bony, Uncle Edward, Grandpa and I gathered round while she read the letters out loud:

September 3, 1942

My Dear Mama and Papa,

I guess by now you know I joined the Navy. We landed on Guadalcanal August 7. The Japs hit us by sea and air. Losses have been heavy but we're holding our own and the Navy has kept us pretty well supplied. Don't worry about me. I'm well as can be expected.

Papa, don't let Ethel sell the cow but if you need to you can slaughter it. Don't go hungry. If you can visit Roy Junior, tell him I'll come for him when the war is over. I pray it ends soon.

God Bless & Keep You,

Roy

August 8, 1942

Dear Mae and Albert,

When you see Betty tell her I'm sorry I didn't say goodbye. I couldn't bear to see her cry with the baby on the way and all. Tell her I got called to duty. I was deployed to Guadcanal. Our job is to protect the sea from the Japanese.

Tell Betty I love her and my darling daughter. I pray the baby arrived safe. Tell Betty to write and send me her address so I can write to her.

All my love,

Merle

Aunt Bony whispered, "See? Your daddy loves you. He's fighting the war. He's a hero."

Grandmommy raised her hand towards heaven, "Thank you, Jesus," she said.

When the dark blue car with US Navy plates turned the corner, Uncle Edward came running. "Mama!" he said, before he lost his tongue. He went to the window and pointed.

Grandmommy slammed the door shut and locked it. "Marisla, close the drapes. Albert, we still haven't heard from Ralph!" She fell to her knees. "Lord God Almighty," she pleaded, "Please don't take my boy. In the name of sweet Jesus, don't take Ralph."

Aunt Bony pushed the drapery aside and peeped out the window. "Gee whiz, Papa," she whispered hoarsely, "he stopped."

"Holy Mary, Mother of God." Grandpa prayed, forgetting that Grandmommy taught him how *not* to be a Catholic years before. He made the sign of the cross.

I heard the clock ticking, then a knock at the door. Aunt Bony covered her ears. Uncle Edward picked me up, put both arms around me and hugged me tight as a bear protecting a fist full of honeycomb. "No. No," he whispered over and over. Another knock. Grandpa hesitated at the door before he cracked it open. The fancy dressed Navy man asked for Margaret O' Reilly. Grandpa pointed across the street.

Grandmommy dropped her head. "Oh Lord, not Frankie."

From the window, Margaret O' Reilly saw Bad News walking across the street, opened the door and screamed, "Go away! I won't be needing to see the likes of you in this house!"

The Navy man said what he came to say, then walked stiffly to the car and drove away.

Grandmommy hurried across the street. Knocked. No answer. At suppertime she took a plate of chicken and dumplings across the street. The drapes were drawn. The thin, gray cat cried to be let in. Grandmommy knocked but the now childless widow wouldn't come to the door. Grandpa fed the scraggly cat. It was the same the next day and the day after that.

On the fourth day, dressed in our Sunday clothes, we waited, hushed, while Grandmommy walked across the street, Bible in hand. This time, Margaret O' Reilly opened the door and stepped out, dressed in black.

At the cemetery, Margaret O' Reilly took the flag from the young man with the white gloves, carefully laid it on the lawn, hiked up her skirt, pulled down her panties and peed on it. "Piss on it," she screamed, "Piss on the sonofabitchin'war!"

The garden was dead and covered with snow. There were no more chickens to put in the pot. Or rabbits. A while back Grandpa had done some work for a man who gave him a sheep and we ate mutton. Roasts. Chops. Then, Grandmommy ground the mutton, mixed it with rice, rolled up in cabbage leaves, and steamed it. Now, all that was left of Grandpa's mutton was a sheep's head.

After church, Grandmommy put the sheep's head in a pot, covered it with water, added minced onion, garlic, and oregano, and set it to boiling.

Grandpa sat by the fire whittling. He sniffed the air. "Smells good, Hon."

Grandmommy sat down next to Grandpa and picked up her crochet. "It's the last of the mutton," she said. "We sure did get a lot of good meals outta that sheep."

Aunt Bony, her bony knees peeping out from under the wool tweed skirt Grandmommy had sewn from one of Grandpa's old suits, plopped down on the floor, tucking in her bare feet, her knees sticking out at an angle like a grasshopper. She spread the Sunday funnies out on the floor and read out loud. She was reading *Little Orphan Annie* when there was a knock at the door.

The preacher, a fat, jolly man with a smile that took up his whole face, and his wife had come unexpected. It being the Lord's Day, Brother MacDonald still wore his Sunday suit. He had no overcoat. He was covered with snow and shivering. The preacher's wife, a little bitty thing, was wearing a thin brown coat that was way too big. On her head was a kerchief made from a flour sack folded in half diagonally and tied under her chin, which made her small white face look even smaller. "We brought a pie, Mae. That's the last of our apples."

"Thank you kindly. Y'all come in."

Grandpa put down the wooden bird he was whittling and moved a chair closer to the fire. "Come. Sit by the fire. Warm up." The preacher's wife sat stiffly on the edge of the chair and leaned towards the fire, rubbing her hands together.

"What smells so good?" the preacher asked in the big, booming voice he used at the pulpit.

"Mutton and dumplings," Grandmommy answered. "Won't y'all stay for dinner?"

Uncle Edward came in the door, carrying an armload of firewood, his black hair now white with snow. He rubbed his bare hands together. You could see his sleeves were way too short. "How do you do?" he said to the preacher, his voice starting out deep and ending in a cackle. His face red, he ducked into the hallway.

Grandmommy turned to the preacher's wife. "Will you excuse me while I check on dinner?"

"I'll help."

"No. No. Sit."

Gwendolyn crawled after Grandmommy, her little blue bloomers peeking out from under her matching ruffled dress. The preacher's wife smiled. "That child looks like a little cherub. You should call her Angel," she said. And the name stuck.

I went into the kitchen to see what Grandmommy was doing in there with that sheep's head. Grandmommy raised the lid and I peeked into the pot. "Look!" I said, pointing to a dumpling in the open mouth of the sheep's head. Grandmommy put her finger to her lips. "Shhhh!"

"But that sheep's head is eating the dumplings."

"Hush your mouth."

I wondered how Grandmommy expected to keep the sheep's head a secret from the preacher and his wife. After all, a sheep's head *is* a sheep's head.

Grandmommy lifted the sheep's head out of the pot and reached for a carving knife. "Go wash up," she said sharply.

A few minutes later, Grandmommy called, "Y'all come to the table. Dinner's ready." Grandpa took his place at the head of the table and motioned for the preacher and his wife to sit. After the blessing, Grandmommy lifted the cover on the casserole and served mutton and dumplings, just like she said.

There was no sign of the sheep's head.

———————◆———————

I didn't talk while we ate supper. If I did, Grandpa would say, "Children should be seen and not heard," and Grandmommy would say, "Don't talk with your mouth full."

Aunt Bony talked plenty. "Mama," she drawled, "Betty told me you took in ironing during the depression so she could take piano lessons so she could make a joyful noise unto the Lord. Aren't you mad that she's got her fingers dancing across the piano in Las Vegas?"

Grandpa stabbed his fork into a potato. "She's got no business off gallivanting."

Grandmommy glared at Aunt Bony, "Marisla, you talk more than a magpie juiced up on elder berry juice."

"Well, aren't you mad? Her off in Vegas, thinking she's gonna be somebody?"

"The Lord gave Betty Lou the gift of music. Praise God. Let her use it to keep the wolf from the door."

Grandpa scowled. "Plenty of wolves in Las Vegas," he mumbled, stirring the food on his plate until it turned into a soupy mess.

Grandmommy said, "Albert, let's pray." She took hold his hand. "Lord, thank you for providing Betty Lou with a job in these hard times. Thank you, Lord, for the money she sends us. In the name of Jesus, Amen."

Grandpa didn't say any more about Las Vegas but when we ate the chocolate pudding Grandmommy made with the cocoa Mama's money bought, he said he didn't want any.

"Hon, I got a WPA[2] job in Utah," Grandpa said. "I want you to come with me. You call Betty. Tell her she needs to come home and take care of the girls."

"Gee whiz, Papa. I can watch 'em," Aunt Bony said.

Grandmommy wrinkled her forehead. "Absolutely not. School starts next week. You and Edward will be gone all day. Betty will have to come home.

But Mama did not come home. She convinced her other sister, Alberta, who was just getting over a broken marriage, to come and help take care of me and Angel.

Alberta was nineteen. She had black hair, skin the color of cream and haunting sea-green eyes. She looked at you directly, as if she wanted to know everything about you. Alberta was pleasingly plump, the most voluptuous of the sisters and the most tenderhearted. She loved children and could be counted on to care for the young, the old, the sick and the dying.

In the spring of 1943, when I was three and Angel a toddler, Mama married a man by the name of Jake Calloway and brought him home.

"I don't like him," Aunt Bony said. "Who does he think he is, with that oily, slicked-back hair parted in the middle, his shirtsleeves rolled up." She made a face. "Gee whiz, he wears striped trousers and suspenders."

Aunt Alberta rolled her eyes. "He's lazy. He sleeps until noon."

Uncle Edward shook his head. "He's a coward. He should be fightin' the war."

---

2. Franklin D. Roosevelt's Work Projects Administration

If he couldn't find a card game, Jake sat bent over the kitchen table smoking cigars, drinking whiskey, and playing pinnacle with Mama. Once in a while, he would raise his head and glance around the room like a hawk looking for prey. He was a cantankerous bully. We took long walks in order to avoid him. Aunt Alberta and Aunt Bony would pile me and Angel into the wooden wagon Grandpa had built and, with Uncle Edward pulling the wagon along behind them, walked all the way downtown. If they had money they'd buy tobacco, orange pop and vodka and sit on the front lawn of the Funeral Hall and smoke and drink until the undertaker came out and said, "Move along."

When we were inside the house, we kept quiet and tried to stay out of Jake's way.

In June 1944, the WPA program ended and Grandpa and Grandmommy returned from Utah. Mama trotted out Jake, hoping Grandpa would approve. Grandpa sat with his arms crossed, his right leg crossed over his left. The right leg twitched like he might be getting ready to kick somebody. Grandmommy brought him a spoonful of soda to settle his stomach. Aunt Alberta brought his fiddle. The fiddle started out loud and angry but before long, Grandpa's frown left, and his face crinkled at the corners of his eyes and mouth. Songs flew off the fiddle. Now the fiddle was a train, chugging along, then speeding up. I jumped up and danced faster and faster, twirling round and round. The fiddle whistled like a train— a long drawn out low pitched, "Whoooo! Whoooo!" I fell to the floor, laughing.

That night, while everyone else slept, Mama and Jake had words. The way it was told to me, one thing led to another and Jake doubled up his fist and hit Mama square in the face. Next thing she knew, his hands were around her throat. Mama tried to pound on the wall to call for help but after only one thump Jake pulled her away from the wall and threw her to the floor.

No telling what Jake would have done if Grandpa hadn't heard that thump. He flung open the door and landed one swift kick right where it counted. Jake curled up like a possum. His eyes rolled back in his head and the pupils disappeared. The eyes came back just in time for Jake to see the claw hammer in Grandpa's hand. He ducked, and the hammer came down hard on his right shoulder. Jake went out the door, bent over, both hands to his crotch, and made his way down A Street with Grandpa waving the hammer in the air and yelling, "Don't come back here, you no good *goat*!"

Grandpa used only three cuss words: dad-burned, whipper-snapper and goat. Other men knew worse words to humble a man but none swore more effectively, nor with the fury, with which Albert Vattell spat out *goat*!

After Grandpa ran off Jake Calloway, it seemed like nothing suited Mama. She was cranky. Fidgety. She smoked day and night. We all knew it wouldn't be long before she took off again. We weren't surprised when she left. We were used to it now. It no longer mattered to me whether she stayed or went.

"Where'd she go?" Aunt Bony asked Aunt Alberta.

"Vegas, I reckon, or Bremerton. Maybe San Francisco."

"Gee whiz, why'd she go?"

"Betty goes where the money is."

―――――――――――――・――――――――――――

The following year, Mama got it in her head that she wanted to bring Aunt Alberta, Aunt Bony, Angel and me on a vacation before Aunt Bony had to go back to school. Next thing I knew, we were on a Greyhound. The bus crept along like a lackadaisical caterpillar crawling from Grants Pass to San Francisco.

A man on the bus had a newspaper and, every now and then, somebody would pass us a page. Mama would read the parts she found interesting out loud. "The war rages unbridled," it said on the front page. Mama laughed. "Now, do you suppose a *'bridled'* war would be any better?"

Aunt Alberta said sadly, "Did you ever think we'd see such hard times?"

"Oh," Mama said, "I've seen hard times before, you know. Depression."

Aunt Alberta shook her head. "This is *war*."

"Gee whiz, Betty, men earn medals for *killing*."

"Yeah. Or *dying*."

Aunt Alberta pointed out the window. "Look at 'em." The bus was driving through a town now, and there was a long line of people- old men, women, and children, winding all around the Catholic church.

"What are they doing?" I asked.

"Waiting for the soup kitchen to open."

They waited silently, their heads hung low like puppets with their strings broken.

In Mama's mind, there was no better way to prove to her sisters that she was on her way to becoming somebody than to bring them to the big city.

"Gee whiz, Betty, you sure do know your way around Frisco," Aunt Bony said as Mama hailed a taxi and told the driver to drive us across the Golden Gate. Mama was as proud of that bridge as if she'd built in with her own two hands.

Then we took a trolley to Coney Island. There was ocean was all around us. There were lots of boats, side by side, as far as we could see, almost as many boats as people. The people were all colors. I took a deep breath, breathing in the salty air and other strange smells. Cotton candy. Fried bread.

Along Fisherman's Wharf we saw seals basking in the sun. A brown pelican stood on the pier. Mama pointed to Alcatraz across the bay. "Gee whiz, that's where they lock up bad people," Aunt Bony told me. Mama insisted we try funny sandwiches called "hot dogs" even though they were 5 cents each.

Too soon, the sun set, painting the clouds pink and orange. Night fell. Gaudy neon signs materialized all around us, the boats lit up, and the lights were reflected on the water, a magical phosphorescent sea. We took a gondola ride, rode horses on the Merry Go Round, ate cotton candy and headed back to the hotel.

Most days, Mama slept half the day, then after she had her coffee, the three sisters sat the card table Mama had arranged to have brought to the room. They played Rummy, smoked cigarettes, and drank whiskey. On her days off, she took us to the movie theater, or to exotic places like Chinatown and Little Italy where the people talked funny. She ordered strange foods, like Chicken ala King, Chow Mein, and Steak Diablo. All the while, telling her wide-eyed sisters stories that always began, "I was being *the great Betty*, you know, when...."

When darkness fell, I lay staring at the ceiling and refused to sleep. Finally, in exasperation, Mama said, "Oh, you can sleep with Alberta and Bones." Terrified that something might happen to Angel, I still wouldn't close my eyes. Aunt Alberta moved Angel's crib next to the bed, so I could watch Angel sleep but after all that I still had nightmares, and no one knew why.

The nightmares were always the same:

> *A little man points his finger at me. He's about one foot tall, and the arm that points is much longer than you would expect, and all around the finger are concentric circles in many colors, radiating out from the finger. The colors spin round and round, swirling faster and faster. At first the circles are small. Then they get larger*

and larger until they encircle me, and I fall
spinning and falling into the spiraling funnel,
faster and faster towards the little man.

Years later, for one flickering moment, I sometimes saw a picture in my mind, a shadow in the night and felt an overwhelming sense of terror. A flash of memory. A shadow in the next room, hovering over Angel's crib. The rest of the picture in my mind is blacked out.

They tell me Clay Stout was there.

4

"Jeepers, that's some jalopy," Uncle Edward said, as a shiny green car pulled up. A pretty woman climbed out. I thought maybe she was lost and looking for direction. She fluffed her hair and patted the hat that looked like a blue cantaloupe rind turned upside-down up top her head. It was sitting cock-eyed on her frizzed up red hair, so the feather stuck on it looked just right. She ran her hands over her blue dress with green polka dots. She was all dressed up like she was headed to prayer meeting. Maybe not. Her mouth was painted, and her eyebrows were plucked. She'd have stuck out like a sore thumb amongst all those Pentecostal sisters.

Grandmommy recognized her right off even though a year had gone by since we had seen her. "Praise God. It's your mama." Mama? Mama had *red* hair!

"She's drivin' a '41 Chevrolet. Special Deluxe. Sport Sedan. Two tone," Uncle Edward said. "They go for eight hundred bucks. *If* you can find one, How'd Betty get a car like that?" [3]

---

3. No cars were manufactured during the war. Scrap metal was collected and used by the military. Automobile companies made tanks and other equipment needed for battle.

"Gee whiz, she's got somebody with her," Aunt Bony said. Mama held up her left hand to show that she had a ring on her third finger. Mama had brought home *another* husband.

Grandpa mumbled something I couldn't make out.

Clayton Stout walked towards us with his head thrust forward, his long skinny arms held out to his sides with the elbows bent. With the sun behind him, he looked like a giant shadowy rooster strutting toward us. When he got close, he let out a whistle and swallowed hard. Twice. I know for sure. I saw his Adam's apple bob both times. "You're darling," he said to Angel and me. "Perfect." He ran his fingers through his hair, causing some to fall across his forehead and cover one eye. The other eye was light brown and flecked with gold, more yellow than not. I had seen eyes like that before. Once, when a rattlesnake slithered into the hen house, Grandpa chopped off its head so it couldn't get the chickens. Clay's eyes reminded me of that rattler.

Mama was hanging onto Clay's arm, parading him around like he was something special. "You can call him 'Daddy' if you want, you know." I shook my head.

Clay put his hands on Mama's waist, lifted her feet off the ground and swung her round. "You've made me the happiest man in the world," he said. "This little family is the best thing that ever happened to me." Clay got down on his haunches and pulled Angel and me close. "I love you girls. Daddy Clay is gonna take care of his girls." He tried to plant a slobbery kiss on my mouth. I turned my head and my cheek got wet.

"Y'all, come sit while I see about supper," Grandmommy said, motioning towards the rocking chairs on the porch. The grownups sat on the porch, sipping sweet tea. I sat on the steps where I could see and hear things. Aunt Bony sat on the railing, dangling her bare feet. Mama shook her head, like she was disgusted. "Where are your shoes? You're *seventeen*. You can't go barefoot your whole life."

"Why not? I like the feel of grass between my toes. I don't like my feet squished up."

"Do you even have decent shoes?" Mama stuck out her foot to show what a proper shoe looked like.

Aunt Bony giggled. "I'm never gonna wear high heels," she said. "Standin' on tip toe. Traispin' round like the Queen. I got penny loafers. I wear 'em downtown and to church. Can't see the need for shoes at home."

Mama opened her mouth to say something but Grandpa frowned, so she let it go.

We sat without talking, watching Angel running around the yard. Clay couldn't take his eyes off her. "Sure is a pretty little thing," he said. "hair the color of corn silk and just as fine."

Angel struggled to climb onto the tire swing. The momentum of her effort pushed her up onto the tire and through it, sending her tumbling head over heels to the ground. The expression on her face was first one of surprise, then sheer happiness. "Me do somersault!" she squealed, clapping her pudgy little hands. "Somersault again." She put her head down and stuck her purple flowered butt up in the air but couldn't remember what came next.

"Would you look at that," Aunt Bony drawled, "Where did she get those purple bloomers?"

"Flour sacks," Grandmommy said." [4]

"Well, I'll be damned."

"Marisla! Watch your mouth."

It seemed like Mama was glad when Aunt Bony put Angel and me to bed. I wished I hadn't sat so close for so long, or maybe I talked too much because whenever I said, "Mama, Mama," she said, "whatta, whatta," like she was mocking me. I could be wrong because after Aunt Bony tucked us in, Mama brought us store-bought teddy bears and kissed us good night before she joined the grownups in the living room.

---

4. During the war, cloth was scarce. When General Mills realized that the poor were using flour sacks for fabric, they printed floral patterns on them.

Peeking out the door, I saw Mama carry her coffee into the kitchen, take a silver flask from her purse, pour something in her coffee, then go back to the living room. Even straining my ears, I couldn't hear what they were saying so I snuck out of bed, pretending to get a drink of water. I could tell Clay was anxious to get on Grandpa's good side. He was talking about his government job and how much money he made. I could see that even putting his best foot forward he wasn't impressing anybody, except Mama. She was laughing too loud, grinning at Clay, acting the fool. Grandmommy's lips were pinched together. Grandpa sat with his arms crossed, his right leg crossed over the left one, jerking up and down like he was ready to kick somebody.

Grandmommy got Grandpa a spoonful of soda to settle his stomach. She stretched and yawned. "Hon," she said, "I think I'll turn in." Since Grandpa and Grandmommy went to bed together and at the same time, Grandpa followed her into their bedroom.

Then Mama came into the bedroom that Aunt Bony shared with me and Angel. "Look, see what good clothes I have." She opened her suitcase, unzipped her dress, let it drop to the floor and pranced around in black lace panties and bra, slipping on first one new dress and then another so Aunt Bony could admire the fine clothes.

"Well, gee whiz," Aunt Bony said, hugging Mama. "Where'd you get 'em?"

"I told you I'd be somebody someday." Mama reached into her purse, I hoped to give Aunt Bony a surprise. But it was only to get papers and tobacco for making cigarettes. No one was allowed to smoke in Grandmommy's house. Mama did it anyway, holding her cigarette in a long silver cigarette holder. Keeping her pinky crooked, she puckered up, making a fish mouth and blew smoke rings at Aunt Bony.

"Betty, where'd you meet Clay?"

"Vegas. He's crazy about me, you know." Mama picked up the purse that was made out of something dead. "He bought me *this*. It's genuine lizard-skin."

"Gee whiz. Where'd you get the car?"

"Clay bought it for me."

"Where'd he get the money?"

"He's got a big job starting up, you know, and needed his money to set it up so I lent it to him. He'll pay me back out of his first paycheck. It's a big-shot job. Money's no problem."

"How come he's not fighting the war?"

"Oh, his job is too important. It's with the *Government*, you know."

"Well, gee whiz. What does he do?"

"Bones, you ask more questions than a prosecuting attorney. No need for you to bother yourself. Clay's *different*. I showed him a picture of the girls, you know, to see what he'd say, and he fell in love with 'em. He'll be a great daddy."

I sat straight up in bed. "Clay's not my daddy. My daddy's coming back."

"That drunken ole Swede? He's *not* comin' back. You get to sleep. Shut your eyes."

Mama got up to leave. "I picked a good one this time. Clay told me he feels like a kid in a candy store with such a perfect little ready-made family. He says he always wanted a little girl of his own." Mama paused at the door, leaned one hand on the doorframe, hiked up her skirt so her thigh showed and stuck her butt out like she was some kind of pin-up girl.

"Well, I'll be damned."

⸻ ◆———◆———◆ ⸻

Next day, Mama and Clay went to Piggly Wiggly to get sugar, if they had any, and coffee. Mama took the little war ration book that Grandmommy took as good care of as she did her Bible. It held stamps needed to buy meat, sugar, cheese and coffee.

As they drove down the driveway, Grandmommy looked up from her crochet. "Clay doesn't wipe his feet before he comes in the house."

"His boots is too big," I said. "He makes too much noise when he walks."

Grandmommy patted me on the head. "Out of the mouths of babes."

Aunt Bony said, "Well, he talks nice. But I don't trust him."

"He's got yellow eyes," I said.

Grandpa scowled. "He's got a yellow streak down his back. Dad-burned coward."

Uncle Edward shook his fist. "Any man worth two cents would be fightin' the war."

"He's got *yellow* eyes," I said. It seemed like nobody else saw what I saw in Clay's eyes. That night, the window was left open on account of the heat, and I could hear voices coming in the window. I climbed out of bed, went to the window, and knelt down. Aunt Bony was already there, her elbows resting on the sill. In the moonlight, we could see Mama and Clay sitting in the car. Mama took a drink from a whiskey bottle and passed it to Clay. Clay took a swig. "Absolutely not," I heard him say. "They're coming with us!"

"Mama don't mind keeping 'em. We can come get 'em once we're settled."

Clay took Mama's face in his hands. "Betty," he said, "Nothing or nobody is gonna keep us apart. I love the girls. They're coming with us, and that's final."

"Oh, boy," Aunt Bony whispered. "Betty don't let nobody boss her. You watch. She's gonna haul off and slap Clay across the face and say, 'Who do you think you're talking to?'"

It was nothing like that. Mama giggled. "You're the boss," she said.

I sucked in air. "I don't want to go gallivanting with Mama and Clay."

Aunt Bony wiped her eyes on her shirt tail. "Get some sleep," she said.

I held my magic quilt tight, shut my eyes, and whispered, "Make Clay go away." Lucky for me, the quilt granted my wish. Next morning, Clay was gone. And so was Mama.

5

Mama and Clay didn't stay gone long enough. They came back a month later to fetch me and Angel. We had been driving across the map, picking apples with the migrants. The migrant's hands moved like hummingbird wings, picking fruit off the trees and putting it in baskets hanging from their necks. Nobody talked. I tried to talk to a little girl. Her mama told me, "Quit foolin'. Run along."

At the end of the day the migrants stood silently, holding their hats in their hands, waiting for pay, then lined up at the company store to buy food and to pay for a place to sleep. Mama said, "Look at 'em, standing in line to pay way too much for their food. And the sad thing is they can't even go where they're not cheated 'cause they're in debt to the company store."

We got in the Chevy and drove to a different store where the food cost less, then went back and rented a tent for the night. Angel looked around the empty space. "We don't got beds."

"We sleep on the floor." It seemed like Mama's mouth was trying to cry but she wouldn't let it.

Angel and I were tickled pink, tucked away in cozy candlelight but when night fell, the tents glowed in the darkness like overgrown lanterns lighting the way for the boogeyman.

"Angel," Mama said, "C'mon over here. Let me give you a cat bath."

"What?"

"Never mind. Take off your clothes."

Angel was standing there, naked and pink, while Mama wiped dirt off with damp washcloth. Angel was swinging her dimpled little rump in time to the music coming out Mama's mouth.

Mama sang low down in her throat and real slow, sometimes catching a word in her throat, holding on to it and then throwing it out, so that even perfectly ordinary words were made to sound mean and naughty. Mama was making up a song of her own:

> My back is aching, and my feet are sore.
> I ought to toss that man right out the door.
> He promised me pearls and a diamond ring.
> Instead,
> He taught me how to sing-ing
> the blues.
> I'm singing the blues, singing blues.

The tent was small. Clay was too near. He was sitting in the corner, staring at Angel with eyes glazed over, like they were hot and feverish. He reeked of sweat. Whiskey. He stuck out the tip of his tongue and ran it across his upper lip. "Mama," I whined, "Clay sticked his tongue out at Angel, and he's looking at her."

Mama turned to look at Clay. Clay stuck his tongue out all the way, stuck his thumbs in his ears and flapped his hands. Angel giggled.

Mama laughed. "Honey," she said, "Why don't you go out to the car and get the sandwich stuff? And I could sure use a drink."

Clay gave me a hard look as he went. I shivered. "Mama," I said, "I don't like Clay looking at me and Angel."

"Well, he's your daddy now. You'll get used to him *looking* at you." Nobody understood what I was trying to tell about the peculiar way Clay looked at Angel and me.

Clay came back with baloney, bread and whiskey. Mama grinned and winked. "I want you to quit *looking* at these girls, you hear?" I could tell she thought it was some kind of joke.

"Okay, I won't *look* at 'em." Clay put his hands over his eyes, laughing like a fool, and peeked out at us between his fingers.

We kept on working crops, putting gas in the Chevy, and driving to a different crop. In Arizona we picked pecans. We ate dates and prickly pear candy. We saw the Grand Canyon and the Petrified Forest. In California we picked oranges. In the Redwood Forest we drove through a hole in a giant tree trunk.

When we stopped for gas, Mama would take Angel and me into the restroom, wipe the dust off us, fill the sink with hot water and wash our clothes. The wrung-out clothes hung out the car in the rolled-up window. That's the way they dried. Mama would say, "We might not be rich, but we can still be clean. We have to look respectable, you know, so we'll be welcome at road stops, unlike the migrants."

Mama chewed on her lip. "I feel sorry for the migrants."

"What are we?"

"Shhh."

When apples were ready to pick in Idaho, we headed north, stopping in Reno where Mama got a two-night gig playing piano for the gold miners. We spent so much time on the road that I learned to read billboards. I read out loud, "Stop. Snake pits. $2. Stop."

Angel said, "Stop. I want to see snakes."

Clay said, "No. It costs too much."

"Stop," I read. "See the giant rattler."

Clay said, "No."

"Stop. Free. Real Live Snakes. Wild Bill's Trading Post and Snake Pit. Free."

Mama said, "All right. All right."

Wild Bill kept the rattlers in a large wooden pen with high sides. Clay lifted us up to see the scary snakes slithering and sliding, some twisted together, wiggling and squirming. "It's feeding time," Clay whispered. "If you don't do what I say, we'll come back here and I'll feed them snakes some little girls."

Angel and I ran took off running. We didn't stop until we were inside the car, hunkered down in the back seat, hiding under a quilt. Angel had the shivers. I had a stomachache. It felt like the devil had reached down in my belly and squeezed.

I knew now that Angel and I were in a heap of trouble.

6

It was August 14, 1945. I was five years old. We were driving across the scorched Arizona desert. Clay was at the wheel, cussing the heat. Mama was fanning herself with a travel map, humming along with Frank Sinatra. Angel was flushed and sweaty, whimpering 'cause she was hot. Mama handed her a cracker. "Stop whining. Nothin' worse than a whiny kid."

"Angel, listen," I said, "I'll read you Burma Shave."[5]

**MANY A WOLF
IS NEVER LET IN
BECAUSE OF THE HAIR
ON HIS
CHINNY-CHIN-CHIN
BURMA-SHAVE**

5. Back then, Burma Shave advertised by placing signs along the highway every so often, each one with one line of a rhyme.

Cracker crumbs stuck to Angel's sweaty little dimpled chin. She ran her hand along her chin. "The woof can't get me 'cause I got hair on my chinny chin chin," she said, giggling.

I wiped her chin. "That's right. The wolf can't get Angel."

Frank Sinatra stopped singing right in the middle of a song. The man on the radio said, "The Japanese surrendered! The war is over!"

Mama grabbed Clay's arm, nearly causing us to go off the road. "The war's over!" Mama bounced up and down. "The war's over. My brothers are done fighting."

"You're shitting me. Well, there goes my government job. Now I won't get paid."

Mama tried to keep her mouth straight. It got lop-sided anyway. "I wonder if Mama and Papa have heard from Ralph. They got letters from Matt and Roy but none from Ralph, last I heard."

"Better stop for gas," Clay said, as he pulled into a filling station out in the middle of nowhere, the first we'd seen in miles and nothing else in sight except heat rising from the pavement in nearly invisible wavy lines.

A one-legged man on crutches hopped quickly out to pump gas. "Did you hear?" He grabbed Clay's hand and pumped vigorously. "The war's over. We got those sonofabitching Japs on their knees. Should've dropped the A-Bomb on them sonsofbitches sooner. See what they done to me?" He lifted half a leg. "We showed them slant-eyed bastards. We showed 'em!"

Clay paid the man and started the car.

"Wait," the one-legged man said. He went inside, still mumbling about the Japs. He returned with a box of chocolate bars. "Here." He handed me the box. "Bet you ain't had one of these in a while."

I handed the box back. "Grandmommy told me not to take candy from strangers."

Mama pinched me and hissed, "Take 'em."

I shook my head. The one-legged man gave the box to Mama. "Here Ma'am, you take 'em. The war's over!" He didn't even ask for our gas stamps.

TESTED
IN PEACE
PROVEN IN WAR
BETTER NOW
THAN EVER BEFORE
BURMA-SHAVE

After driving miles and miles through wheat stubble, we ended up somewhere in Idaho. Clay turned onto a dusty dirt road and brought the Chevy to a stop at the foot of a hill.

The large white two-story house sat up on the rise, bathed in white moonlight. One big black tree stood in front of the house and off to the right. We walked up the twisting path and climbed six steps onto a wide porch with a banister all around. We crossed the porch and waited. Clay's mother opened the door. Stern, tight-lipped, she turned and went back inside. We followed her into the kitchen. She motioned for us to sit, made ham sandwiches, and poured milk. She seemed tired, as if just seeing us had worn her out.

We had been there close to twenty minutes when the door opened with a bang and Clay's sister barged in. "You are not welcome here," she yelled at Clay, waggling her finger in his face. Now she jerked her thumb towards Mama, "Where'd you get *her*?" She turned to face Mama and hollered, "You go right back where you came from. Clay does not need to be mixed up with a woman with two little girls. Did he tell you he's got a little girl of his own he can't see?"

Mama stood up. "Let's go. I won't stay where I'm not wanted."

Clay's mother sighed. "Stay the night. Have a bath. Get a good night's sleep before you leave. The little girls look tired."

We were tired. Mama was, too. It had been close to a month since we'd slept in a bed.

Mama sat back down. Clay's mother led Angel and me upstairs. We climbed into bed, lying close together, feeling out of place in a strange bed. Clay's mother stood at the foot of the bed, glaring at us with mean eyes, same as Clay's, then turned and walked away.

Angel scooted closer and whispered in my ear, "I heared a scary noise."

We listened, straining our ears. Something scratched at the window, trying to get in. We scrunched down and pulled the covers tight around us. The scratching was getting louder. A monster was trying to open the window! We pulled the covers down real slow and peered at the window, straining our eyes.

Angel saw it first. "Look!" She pointed.

"What?"

The scratching came again. Angel dove under the covers. I stared at the window, squinting, trying to make out what was scratching. Then I saw it- a bony arm. A bloody fist knocked at the window! I grabbed Angel's hand and we ran screaming down the stairs. Once we calmed down enough to tell, Mama went outside to investigate. I figured we'd most likely never see her again.

After a long time, Mama came back, followed by twin boys about fifteen years old. "I met your brothers," she said to Clay, "and I've captured the monster." At the same time, she brought her hand from behind her back. In it was the monster's arm, the bloody hand still attached. Angel howled like a wolf cub and jumped up and down, stomping her feet. I closed my eyes, held my breath, and screamed.

"Stop it!" Mama grabbed me by the shoulders and shook me so hard my teeth clattered against each other. "Stop it. Look."

I opened one eye, and then the other, my heart knocking against my rib cage. The monster's arm was long and skinny. I shut my eyes and screamed louder.

"Open your eyes," Mama said. "Look."

The monster arm looked like a branch ripped off a small tree. It was wearing a glove. I looked closer. "Look, Angel," I said, much relieved, "It's not a monster. It's only a glove tied to a branch and dipped in red paint."

The grownups laughed and sent us back to bed. I lay awake, staring first at the window, then at the door, anxious to get away from this peculiar house.

Next morning, after breakfast, Mama and Clay took us to visit some people we had never seen before. We sat stiffly, in the seldom used parlor, with Glenny, a short, solid woman with a big flat face and dull eyes. We sat, sipping cold drinks, looking first at our feet, then studying the faded flowers in the paper on the wall.

Mama set down her drink. "Why don't you take the girls out to see the cow, you know?" Glenny took Angel and me by the hand and led us out to the barn where a man sat on a little stool pulling on the cow. Each time he pushed his thumbs in and yanked, milk came out in a thin stream that he directed into the bucket. Sometimes he squirted the milk into the mouth of the orange, white and black kitten sitting on the bale of hay nearby.

After the milking, we ran to the house, anxious to show Mama the kitten. "Mama, Mama," Angel called. "Mama, where are you? Come see the kitty!"

Mama was gone!

Angel put back her head and howled, her body shaking.

Glenny said, "That's enough of that, you little brat. Get to bed before I whup yer butt." She led us into a wallpapered room at the end of the hall. There were two soft beds, identical, with blankets and pillows. Angel climbed into bed with me, threw her arms around my neck and sobbed on my neck, her hair tickling my nose. "Don't cry," I whispered. Giant tears made their way up my throat and spilled out my eyes onto Angel's silky hair.

———◆———

Glenny put a bag of potatoes on the table. "Peel the tators," she said. I stared at the potatoes. I stared at the knife. "I don't know how," I whined. "I'm too little to peel potatoes."

"You're not too little, you're too stupid. You're too slow. You waste too much tator. And you're too tall to be five, you must be six."

Glenny lied. She told the principal that I was six. I started first grade a year early so Glenny wouldn't have to put up with my stupidity.

It was no better at school. Glenny made me wear ugly wool stockings to school. I itched something terrible. I scratched and scratched and scratched. I scratched so hard I drew blood and, when the bloody scratches scabbed over, I clawed off the scabs. I sat at my desk and rubbed my foot against my ankle. I lifted up my skirt and clawed at my crotch.

At recess the kids wouldn't come near me. They pointed and laughed. They chanted in a singsong voice:

"Cooties. Cooties.
Lucinda has cooties.
She can't do her duties
because she's got cooties."

I kept my hurt feelings to myself. Alone at night I cried myself to sleep.

———————————— ✦ ————————————

Four months later, Mama and Clay showed up on Christmas Eve, unexpected, and whisked us off to a Motor Court. "You can't stay overnight, you know," Mama explained, "because there isn't enough room but we'll all go out to supper together, then tomorrow we'll have a good Christmas."

"Are you gonna take us with you when you leave?" Angel asked.

"We'll see," Mama said. I knew then that she'd leave without us.

And now Mama took Angel to the store, leaving me alone with Clay.

"Daddy Clay's little girl looks tired," Clay said. "Come lie down next to Daddy, darling."

"I'm not tired."

"It's time for your nap," Clay said, pulling the drapes shut and locking the door

"I'm too big for a nap."

Clay opened the drawer of the bedside table, took out a seven-inch pig-sticking knife and put it on the table. "Take off your clothes," he said, his voice cold and hard.

I looked at that sharp knife and did like Clay said. I sat on the bed shivering, all goose bumpy. Clay stood in front of me, grinning. He unbuttoned his pocket, reached in and took something out. "Look here at what I got for you." He cradled the pink thing in his hand. "Pet it." I touched it gently. I was thinking, *It's some kind of animal- naked like Grandpa's baby rabbit but I don't see eyes or ears.*

Clay rubbed the thing on my leg. I didn't like seeing that thing, but I kept looking 'cause I didn't know what it might do, maybe bite me or something. The thing got mad and spit at me. Clay put it back in his pocket and buttoned it up. I wasn't sure whether it had teeth or not, but I knew it was a mean thing. I was afraid it might get loose.

"Don't tell nobody what we done, or I'll have to use this." Clay reached for his knife. "Give me your hand," he said. Clay put the knife against my hand and pressed down. I felt something like the sharp sting of a hornet. I stared stupidly at the palm of my hand, watching blood ooze out and drip on the floor.

"Wash up," Clay said.

I was standing next to the sink, scrubbing the leg that wouldn't come clean, when Mama got back. I wiped my wet cheek with the towel.

"Have you been crying?" Mama asked me.

Before I could answer, Clay said, "I spanked her. She was playing with my knife."

"Did not," I said.

"Then how did you do this?" Clay grabbed my hand and held it out so Mama could see the cut. "She cut herself."

Mama grabbed me by the shoulders and shook me. "Never, never touch Clay's knife. It's real, real sharp. You could get killed."

That's what I thought.

I was walking home from school in drizzling freezing rain. School was far, way past the billboard that said, "Lucky Strike Means Fine Tobacco," past the Motor Court, clear through town. Some kids took the shortcut across the pasture, but I was afraid of the bull. And once, when I touched the fence, it buzzed my teeth.

I was walking fast when I saw the Motor Court up ahead, and that got me thinking about the thing Clay had shown me. I was thinking, *It might still be there. It might get loose and come after me. It might bite me.* Hot yellow pee ran down my legs. My panties were squishy, so I took them off and threw them on the ground behind the billboard, then I crawled under the humming fence and ran past the mean bull, taking the shortcut across the pasture, my heart galloping in my chest.

Now every day, when I got almost to the Motor Court, I got to thinking about the thing I had seen. I couldn't stop the pee from soaking my panties and running down my leg. I took off my panties and threw them behind the billboard. Nobody knew until I used up all my underwear and Glenny pulled up my dress and saw I had no panties on. "You little slut!" she screamed, grabbing my shoulders and shaking. "Where are your panties?"

"Behind the billboard."

"You little whore, what do you do behind the billboard?"

"I wet my panties, so I took 'em off."

"Why does a big girl like you pee your pants?"

"I'm scared to walk past the Motor Court. It makes me wet my panties."

"Scared. What are you scared of?" Glenny set her jaw and narrowed her eyes. "Answer me. What are you scared of?"

"Some kind of animal. Like a snake."

"You little liar," Glenny screamed. She leaned me over a chair and took a green willow switch to my bare butt. "You're a filthy, evil little girl. God is gonna send you straight to hell."

Please God, Don't send me to hell. In the name of Jesus. Amen

"Happy Birthday," Mama said over the phone. I had no idea it was my birthday. I was glad to hear Mama's voice but I didn't have much to say. Seeing as how nobody ever believed me, I had pretty much quit talking.

Angel grabbed the phone away from me and told Mama, "Glenny called Lucinda bad names. She said she was evil. She whipped her with a tree, and she told the devil to come get her and put her in hell."

Glenny grabbed the phone. "Get to bed," she yelled. We didn't hear what was said after that.

After the phone call, Glenny came into the room and screamed at Angel. "You're a trouble-making little shitass liar." Then she turned off the night light, leaving us in the dark, and stomped out of the room.

Angel whispered, "*You* a shitass."

"Don't say bad words," I said. Angel was only three. It was my responsibility to teach her right. Secretly, I was proud as all get out.

Angel had gumption.

"Y ou're a poor excuse for a human being," Clay told Glenny. "You ought to be strung up. How could you treat my sweet innocent little girl like that?"

It was midnight. Mama and Clay had come to snatch us away from Glenny. He gathered Angel and me up in his arms and hugged us tight. "Daddy Clay won't leave you ever again," he said. "I love you girls so much."

As Clay carried us out to the car, I saw his Adam's apple bobbing up and down like he was trying to choke back tears. "We got us a house now," he said. "I'm gonna take care of you. You believe me, don't you?" I nodded and put my arms around his skinny neck. Angel kissed him on the cheek.

Castle Rock, Washington 1946
On the roof of the Chevy, under the tarp, were mattresses, a table, four chairs, a broom and a rag mop. From the end of the rag mop dangled

a tin bucket tied on with a red bandana. Mama stood back and looked at the Chevy, chuckling and shaking her head. "What would Mama think?" That's what she always said whenever she did something she thought Grandmommy might not approve of.

Clay cut the rope that held our stuff on and piled everything up near the cabin, took Mama's list and headed for town.

"Wait," Mama yelled, waving both arms so Clay would see her in the rear-view mirror.

Clay backed up. "Now what?"

"The boxes. You forgot the boxes."

"Oh, *I* forgot the boxes. *I* forgot. Well, excuse me. How could I forget it was *my* job?" Clay got like that sometimes. Sarcastic, Mama called it.

I couldn't figure out why Mama wanted a sarcastic man smelling up the place. Sweet talk, I guess. One time, I overheard Grandmommy tell Aunt Bony, "Betty Lou is too young and stupid to know Clay is sweet-talking her."

Clay grabbed the boxes Mama had put on the floor between the front and back seats and threw them on the ground. "There. Or is it my job to carry 'em in, too?"

Mama chewed her lip. She picked up the largest box and struggled under its weight, as the car sped away. She nodded in the direction of two small boxes. "Make yourself useful."

Angel and I picked up the boxes and followed Mama up a little hill. The log cabin was situated a ways back from the road, up the hill and past the well, which was built of stone. When we got to the well, Mama stopped and put down the box. She turned the handle and the rope wound itself around the pulley and raised a wooden bucket of water clear and cold as ice. We drank from a tin cup hanging from a nail. "Never, never go near the well alone," Mama said. "It's too dangerous. You could fall in."

The cabin was small, and tucked under three large pines. Out back was the outhouse, smelly and buzzing with flies. Mama dumped a whole bag of lye in the hole and poured Clorox on the seat. "Leave the door open." She propped the door open with a good size rock. "Let it air out."

Mama stood on a chair and swept the cabin ceiling, knocking down cobwebs and a bird nest, empty except for a small, speckled eggshell, then swept the walls and finally the floor. Then she swished the rag mop across the floor. "Stay outside while the floor dries."

We sat on the steps, looking out over the barbwire fence, across the pasture and past another little cabin. As far as we could see were trees. Our new home was in the midst of a pine forest.

Mama plopped down on the step next to Angel, lit a cigarette and blew smoke rings into the air. "Isn't it beautiful?"

"What?" Angel asked.

"The land. Daddy Clay is gonna buy it, you know. Twenty acres. He's gonna build us a *big* house. I'm gonna be somebody."

The floor was dry and smelling like fresh cut pine. "Give me a hand." Mama was putting brand new sheets on the two iron beds. "The little bed is for you girls, the big one for me and Daddy Clay," she said, as she handed me two patchwork quilts. "Here." I spread the quilts and Angel fluffed the pillows while Mama washed windows and hung curtains.

We brought in firewood and Mama built a crackling fire in the big black stove that sat smack dab in the middle of the one room. From one of the boxes, she took a large, blue-speckled pot and heated water. Angel clapped her hands. "It's comfy. We don't gotta sleep in a tent."

Mama pointed to a large tin washtub. "It's Angel's turn to bathe first," she said. Mama soaped Angel's chubby pink body, scrubbed her hair, wrapped her in a towel, then handed me the soap. "Hurry up and take your bath before the water gets cold."

I stripped down and climbed into the washtub. "The water is cold, Mama."

"Can't be."

"Is, too."

"Let me see." Mama stuck her hand in the water. "It is." She pushed the tub closer to the stove. "Hurry up before you get cold and catch your death." She always said that. She got it from Grandmommy. Even if it was the middle of the summer and you got wet they said it.

I was running the slippery soap over my goose-pimpled body when I felt eyes on me. I turned. Clay was staring at me with those scary eyes. I took a step back and burned my butt on the hot stove. "Ow, ow, ow," I yelped, jumping up and down.

Clay scooped me up and carried me to the smaller of the two beds. "Let me see. Poor little darling. Let Daddy Clay see."

Mama brought the first aid kit in from the car and Clay rubbed ointment on my burned butt, his hands cold and clammy, his eyes shiny.

I wondered why Mama never saw Clay's eyes like I did. When he looked at me, I saw yellow devil eyes. When he looked at Mama she saw something else. It was like Clay was wearing a mask. He grinned at Mama. "Look what I brought the most beautiful woman in the world," he said, handing Mama a heart-shaped box.

"Chocolates!" Mama giggled and wiggled all over like a puppy getting its butt scratched.

Clay held up a brown paper bag. "Come see what Daddy Clay got for his pretty little girls." In the bag were two coloring books, a box of crayons, and a tiny tea set. "Ain't I good to you? Come give Daddy Clay a kiss." Angel threw her arms around Clay's neck and kissed him on the forehead. He was still holding on to the crayons. I grabbed the box with both hands, pecked him on the cheek and pulled it out of his hand. "C'mon, Angel," I said, "Let's color."

Angel and I spread the tea set out on our bed, colored, and sipped pretend tea with our dolls until Mama called us to supper.

Clay took a bite of beef stew and reached for another biscuit. He was working his throat, the Adam's apple bobbing up and down. He had tears in his eyes. "I ain't never been so happy," he said. "The best thing a man can do for hisself is get a family. This here family is the best thing that ever happened to me. I love you all so much. Daddy Clay is gonna take such good care of you. You believe me, don't you?"

Angel and I nodded. Mama leaned over and kissed him.

Clay said, "Tomorrow we start logging. You'll see. I'm gonna take care of my girls."

The sun dropped down behind the trees, and in the light of the kerosene lantern, the cabin had shrunk. The corners had become shadowy places where monsters could hide, and there were black scary caverns beneath the beds.

Angel and I huddled together in our new bed. Angel's head had scarcely touched the pillow when she fell fast asleep. I lay listening to the sound of the wind racing through the trees. The wind crashed into the pines overhead, shaking the branches. The branches creaked, bent down and swished across the tin roof, then the wind whipped around behind the trees and changed direction.

Soon Clay and Mama were making noise like pigs grunting. The moon peeked in the window and saw them naked and wallowing in the bed all tangled together. It was a terrible sight to see. Even the moon couldn't take it and hid its face behind a cloud.

Clay's eyes were looking across the room right at me. I shut my eyes and tried to block out the terrible sight but I couldn't get the awful thing I had seen out of my head. Long after it was over, I lay awake trying to figure why Mama liked wrestling with Clay.

It rained that night. I liked the lively sound of the tinkly rain on the tin roof, like the sound of a thousand little feet scampering overhead. I fell asleep listening.

By morning the rain had gone but I could still hear the sound of little feet. Mama said, "It's probably a rat." Barefoot, I ran out to see for myself. It was wet underfoot where rain had run in riverlets the night before. Mud squished up between my toes. I could hear tree frogs and the chattering of a squirrel.

On the roof was a small gray squirrel, his bushy tail folded over his back. He looked at me with bright eyes, flicked his tail, jumped onto the pine branch that hung over the cabin, scampered up the tree and disappeared.

On my way to the outhouse, I saw Squirrel again. He followed me, jumping from tree to tree. He kept his eyes on me, looking me over, like he was sizing me up. Now he hung upside down, peering intently at my face, then scampered to the ground and sat motionless on his hind legs, chattering at me between buck teeth. He wanted to be friends.

Next day, I left a peanut on the stump of a large oak and sat motionless and waited for Squirrel to find it. I didn't have to wait long. Squirrel scampered down a nearby tree and climbed onto the stump, taking the peanut in his tiny paws and twitching his tail as if to say, "thank you". I reached into my pocket for another peanut but before I could lay it down, Squirrel reached out and took it from my hand. He sat on his haunches like a little old man, nibbling on his peanut.

After that, I brought peanuts every day. Squirrel became my best, my only friend.

Every morning now we woke at dawn and splashed our faces with icy-cold well water. After breakfast Mama dropped Angel at the Buckners, and we went into the woods where Clay logged the land they called the upper twenty.

A bulldozer cut a road, knocking down trees, baby trees and all. The road made a red clay scar all across the green woods. Clay *killed* trees. First, he made a notch in the tree truck. The ax halfway disappeared into the tree. Scattered chips were sticky with tree-blood. Next, Clay cut the tree, using a one-man bucksaw, gave a great big push, yelled, "TIMMBERRR" and ran, 'cause you never knew for sure which way a tree would fall.

No one seemed to think it strange that I spent my days like a wood nymph, tip-toeing through the woods barefoot. I found shy flowers hiding in the shade of lacy green ferns. A bird nest. A salamander under a rock. Blackberries. Wild strawberries. I lay flat on my stomach and drank from the spring. In the clearing past the maple trees, I sat on a moss-covered log, watching a brown-eyed doe and her long-legged speckled fawn eat apples I had strewn on the ground. Sometimes they came quite close.

One day, the baby deer ate from my hand. I reached out and stroked his speckled coat.

It was near noon. Mama had gone back to the cabin to get the liverwurst sandwiches she had made that morning. I sat on the stump, watching Clay kill trees. He worked alone, climbing up trees, cutting off limbs, felling trees so big a full-grown man couldn't put his arms around the trunk. Some said, "He's a hell of a logger, does the work of two men." Others said, "He's a damn fool, working alone in the woods." Mama said, "He's too proud to ask for help."

I sat on the stump and watched Clay notch the tree, then start in with the bucksaw, slowly working it back and forth, back and forth. Every now and then he'd stop and wipe sweat from his forehead with his checkered sleeve, rubbing his arm across his face, then reach for the water bottle and drink, his head back, his skinny neck red and chafed. He wore scratchy checkered wool, even in summer, to protect him from the saw blade should it happen to slip.

I took a sip from my water bottle. That's when I spotted the doe and her baby, barely visible in the dappled shade. I was thinking, *They must've followed me from the meadow They probably smell the apple I brought with me.*

"Oh, no!" I blurted out without thinking.

"What?" Clay wanted to know.

"Nothing," I lied. "A mosquito."

Clay kept sawing away at the tree. The tree shuddered and crashed to the ground, sending scared forest critters running. The frightened doe didn't know which way to turn. She ran *towards* us, the fawn right behind her. *Go away*, I screamed inside my head.

Clay backed up slowly. He had his eye on the gun he always kept close by. It was lying on the ground next to me. I was thinking, *Grab the gun and shoot him. Now!*

Clay beat me to it. He grinned, raised his hand, pointed the gun at the fawn and pulled the trigger.

"Run!" I whispered, "Run!"

The baby deer was so scared she couldn't move. Clay fired another shot. Blood seeped out the baby deer's shoulder and dripped down, turning the ferns red. She staggered, wobbled, and fell. She kicked her long legs and struggled, trying to get up. Finally, she gave up and lay still. She was lying in a pool of blood, her large brown eyes staring straight at me.

I was shaking so hard I could scarcely stand. I said nothing. I had been struck dumb.

Clay nudged me with his left hand, the one with the gun. He pointed it at me. "That's what happens when somebody does what she ain't supposed to do."

Mama wouldn't allow Squirrel in the cabin, and I was pretty sure I'd never get myself a friend, except for Squirrel, on account of I couldn't trust anybody. I started pestering Mama for a pet I could bring inside. "Can I have a pet?" I pleaded. "A kitty?"

At first, Mama acted like she didn't hear me.

"Mama," I persisted, "I really do need a pet to keep me company when you're logging and Angel's at Buckner's."

"Oh, you do, do you?" I could tell, by the look on her face, Mama was weakening.

I stuck out my lower lip. "I'm lonely," I said, expecting Mama to give in.

To my surprise, it was Clay who said, "I'll get you a pet right now." Darned if he didn't get up and jump in the truck like he meant it. "Want to go with me?" Clay called out to me.

I shook my head.

Clay was gone almost an hour. He came back empty handed.

"Where's my kitty?" I wanted to know.

Clay put his hand to his ear. "I think I hear something coming now." A truck pulling a trailer rumbled down the road, backed up the hill and stopped. In the trailer was a horse, a chestnut with black mane and tail. Clay led her to the pasture, opened the gate and let her loose. She galloped to the far corner of the pasture.

"Is she mine? What shall I name her?"

"How about 'Kitty?'"

"Mama!"

"Well, you wanted a kitty. Now's your chance." Mama laughed. "Can't you just see her standing there calling, 'Here Kitty, Kitty, Kitty,' and then this big ole *horse* comes clompin' along?" Mama laughed harder. "Here Kitty, Kitty, and this *big* ole *horse* comes clompin' up."

Seemed to me like Mama was always laughing at my expense, so I came up with an idea that would have her laughing out the other side of her mouth. "I *will* call the horse Kitty," I said.

I stood at the fence calling, "Here, Kitty, Kitty, Kitty." I didn't feel a bit silly calling the big horse "Kitty."

Kitty's job was to drag the logs down the winding mountainside road. Clay used the A-frame he built to lift the logs onto the little red REO Mama drove to the mill. Sometimes, I rode with Mama, feeling warm inside, thrilled to be sitting next to her singing about sunshine making us happy.

You could smell the pulp mill stench miles before you got to the mill. Smelled like something dead. Mama dumped our logs into the river with the other dead trees, where they landed like giant pick-up-sticks. Men in spiked boots walked on the logs in the water, shoving them around with long sticks. When Mama climbed out of the REO, the men ran on the logs to show off, hollering and whistling at her. Mama took no offense. She waved and grinned.

On Sunday Kitty didn't have to work. I would grab hold her mane and climb up on her back, riding bareback up the mountain, past the timberline, where the most tender grass and beautiful wildflowers grew.

I pretty near burst with pride, having such a nice horse for a friend.

I spread peanut butter on raisin bread, covered it with another slice of bread and cut the sandwich this way and that, making nine tiny sandwiches. These I placed in a basket along with the little blue and white tea set and a napkin.

Squirrel waited on the roof until I came out. Now he followed me into the woods, jumping from tree to tree. I carried the picnic basket to my favorite stump, spread the napkin on the stump, filled the teapot with cool water from the spring, and set out the tea set. Squirrel climbed down the tree, scampered up onto the stump, and ate a sandwich from the little china plate.

Blue jay shrieked a warning. Squirrel scooted up a tree. I heard the scary sound of big boots bruising moss and rustling silver birch. Sharp snap of a broken twig.

I tossed the tea set into the basket, tiptoed backwards down the path, hid the basket in the berry brambles, crept under the briars and lay flat against the cool smooth ground.

Clay slithered on by.

8

One day Clay took us to visit his friend who lived across town in a dingy little house that reeked of smoke and urine. Diapers hung from clotheslines crisscrossing the small, dark room. The diapers were hung to dry without having been washed first and the stench was strong. Slices of apple, strung on strings, dried over the wood stove. The apples were covered with flies.

It was too warm. Smoke stung my eyes. I sat on the floor near Mama's feet, keeping my eyes and ears open. The man's wife didn't talk much. She was practically invisible. Something about the man caught my eye. As I watched him and Clay, I could tell they were two of a kind. The men talked fast and loud, excited about their new families. The man bragged about having a baby of his own. Clay jabbed him in the ribs with his elbow and said something about Angel and me that only the man heard. The man laughed and brought out a whiskey bottle. "I'll drink to that."

Somehow, later that evening, I ended up in the bathroom with the man and a baby boy about two months old. The man put the baby on a changing table, took off the baby's diaper and washed his bottom. I leaned over and took the baby's hand. He wrapped his tiny fingers around mine. I wondered, *Why is it taking so long to change a diaper?* I talked to the cooing, smiling baby, no bigger than my doll, waiting for the diaper to be pinned.

A dog, the kind they call a collie, came into the bathroom, her toenails clicking across the floor, the hair on her back raised. She growled at the man. The man grabbed the dog by the scruff of the neck, threw her down the basement stairs and slammed the door, then turned back to the baby. The baby scrunched up his face, stiffened his body, kicked his little legs and let out a screech. I jumped back and knocked over the baby oil.

The dog whimpered and scratched at the basement door.

I bent down to pick up the baby oil and saw something terrible. I ran from the screams, the bad man and the telltale drops of blood on the changing table.

I ran to Mama and whispered what I saw. I crouched down next to Mama, held my breath, and waited to see what Mama would do when she found out this horrible thing.

The bad man came into the room with the crying baby and laid him down in a smelly bassinet across the room. The baby cried and kicked his little legs. Mama turned and glared at the bad man, then went back to her whiskey. I went to the baby and started to pick him up. The bad man said, "Get away from him."

Angel tugged on Mama's shirt. "The baby's crying." Still Mama did nothing.

Mama and Clay sat in the smoke-filled room puffing on cigarettes and drinking whiskey with the man and woman. The baby cried on and on. Still, they drank. They drank and drank and drank. Even after Angel fell asleep on the filthy floor, curled up in a little ball beside the stove, they kept on drinking. I squiggled up next to Angel, put my arms around my knees and rocked back and forth. I shut my eyes real tight and pretended I was far away.

I was in a black place where I couldn't hear the baby cry.

A few weeks later, the man from the dingy house came by and dropped off the collie. "The girls can have the dog," he told Clay. "I got to leave town. They're lookin' for me."

"Is it bad?"

"Real bad."

"Take the logging road," Clay said, "It'll take you all the way to Longview. They won't find you. And it's not far to the state line."

Angel helped me bathe the dog. She grabbed a bottle of what she thought was baby oil and rubbed it on the dog's belly. The dog let out a yelp, took off running and stayed gone three days. "What did you expect?" Mama said, "Eucalyptus burns, you know." She laughed, "You should name the dog 'Eucalyptus'." Angel couldn't say "Eucalyptus" 'cause it was a big word, so we called our new dog "Lyptus".

Lyptus followed me wherever I went, even past the timberline where I rode Kitty. I felt safe, even from Clay, especially since Grandmommy, Grandpa, Aunt Bony and Uncle Edward were coming to spend the summer.

Aunt Bony unwound her lean, lanky body and leapt from the backseat. She was eighteen now and had finally grown breasts! "You little skunk," she drawled. "Look what I brought you." The monkey dolls were made from socks, the gray and white kind that had red heels, so that the monkeys had red butts.

Uncle Edward climbed out of the car. He was sixteen and almost as tall as Aunt Bony. "I'm gonna get you," he teased. Angel took off running and giggling. Uncle Edward caught her, picked her up, put her on his shoulders and galloped up the hill carrying Angel piggyback.

Grandpa swooped me up and rubbed his chin whiskers on my cheek. I could smell peppermint. "Look at 'em, Hon," Grandmommy said, like we were something special.

The next day, while Clay cut trees and Mama hauled them to the mill, I led Grandmommy and Grandpa to the berry patch. "Look," I said, "You can crawl under the briars and hide if you need to." Grandmommy gave Grandpa a look I couldn't make out, then started in picking berries and mumbling something to Lord God Almighty about keeping little girls safe.

That night Grandmommy made blackberry cobbler for supper, and when night fell she covered me with the magic shell quilt she had brought with her. Grandpa tickled me with his chin whiskers, then they headed down the path to their cabin.

I hugged the magic quilt and whispered three wishes, all three exactly the same. *Make Clay stop bothering me!*

⸻

Grandpa built old man Buckner a lean-to for his goat, in exchange for a Jersey cow. "After the calf is born," Grandpa explained, "we'll have all the milk we need." I loved the gentle brown cow. Big eyes. Long eyelashes. Tail swishing flies off her bony butt.

Every afternoon, Grandpa and I herded the cow home, Grandpa calling, "Come, Bossy. Boss. Boss." Then Lyptus learned to bring the cow. Grandpa and I had only to open the gate.

One day, Aunt Bony yelled, "Papa! The calf is comin'."

"How do you know?"

"I saw it's feet stickin' out. Hurry, Papa."

Mama wouldn't let me watch the calf being born. I figured I knew how the cow looked, with stiff little calf feet sticking out her big belly like pins in a pincushion.

After the sweet little calf was born, I crawled into the pen and wrapped my arms around his neck and let him suck my fingers. Mama cow didn't mind. Every now and then she turned and licked my face, her tongue long and prickly. I giggled.

Now I had lots of friends: Mama cow and the calf, Lyptus, Kitty and Squirrel.

It was a good summer except when Clay caught me alone. I learned to watch Clay. Before long, I could sense and sometimes escape his dangerous moods. Still, he sometimes managed to trap me and rub himself up against my bare legs. By day I lived in terror of his evil eyes. At night I was caught up in the terrible dream where the little man pointed his long, long finger at me, and the colors swirled all around me as I fell whirling and spinning into the bottomless pit.

Now Clay spread my magic quilt over a stump and made me sit naked while he did unspeakable things to me with his eyes and things to himself, his breath raspy. He made other sounds like the noises that come from the snout of a hog rooting in the mud. He grinned and his eyes glazed over. He left a trail of slime across the magic shells. I was thinking, *Maybe Clay isn't a man at all, maybe some kind of a devil. Maybe Grandmommy can cast the demon out of my life. Maybe Grandpa can chase him off with a claw hammer.* "I'm gonna tell Grandpa," I threatened. Clay took his knife, stabbed it into the pink shell, and walked away, laughing a mean laugh.

I drug the quilt that had lost its magic to the spring and scrubbed and scrubbed and scrubbed but the quilt still smelled like slime. I brought it to Grandmommy. She took the soggy quilt that had been dragged through the woods and washed it good in hot soapy water and then hung it out in the fresh air to dry. "What happened to your quilt?" she asked.

"Got dirty," is all I said. "Where's Grandpa? I got to tell him something."

"Gone to Grants Pass. He'll be back Sunday."

That night I dreamed: *Rough hands grab me and throw me into the air. I'm falling, falling, falling down, down, down into a large wooden box with high sides. There are snakes in the box, snakes all around me. Snakes! It's dark in the box but I can see yellow snake eyes looking at me. I feel snakes slithering, writhing, sliding across my legs. There is no way to escape the slippery slimy snakes.*

On Saturday, Aunt Bony, Angel and I went with Mama and Clay into town. Aunt Bony was sitting in the backseat with Angel and me, teaching us how to play "I Spy," when Clay turned around, reached over the back seat and fondled her breast. Aunt Bony doubled up her fist and socked Clay square in the face. Then Clay slugged Aunt Bony.

Mama pulled over. "What's going on?"

Quick with his lies, Clay answered without hesitation. "I was trying to get a bee out of the car so it wouldn't sting Angel," he whined. "And Bones hit me for no reason."

"He's fibbing," Aunt Bony drawled, "He pinched my titty so I socked him and the bastard hit me with his fist."

"Bones, don't you tell anybody Clay hit you. Papa would be awful mad. He might kill him."

In spite of what Mama had told her, Aunt Bony wasted no time telling Grandmommy what Clay had done. Grandmommy was mad as all get out. She wasn't scared of nobody, not even the devil. She sure enough wasn't scared of Clay. She took Aunt Bony by the hand, marched up to the cabin and looked Clay straight in the eye. "I've got a bone to pick with you," she said. "You ever lay a hand on my daughter again and I'll beat the tar out of you." Then she whopped Clay upside the head, turned and marched out the cabin.

Clay went for his gun, which he kept under the mattress, and started out down the path after Grandmommy. Scared that Grandmommy might not see Clay lurking in the shadows, I ran to the door to warn her. Mama grabbed me by the hand, drug me across the room and put me on the bed next to Angel. "You stay put."

Uncle Edward, who had been shooting cans off fence posts before it got dark, grabbed his .22 rifle and headed out after Clay.

Aunt Bony started towards the door.

Mama said, "Stay with the girls." Then she fetched a small pearl-handled gun out of the coffee can, which was kept on the shelf on the wood stove, and took off after them.

It occurred to me that one of them might shoot Clay. A smile spread across my face, and then I laughed the high-pitched hysterical laugh of a maniac.

I was hoping Clay would end up dead.

"Let's hide," Angel said, her eyes big and round. We scrunched up into a little ball, our arms around each other. Aunt Bony pulled the covers up over our heads. We lay there, not moving, hardly breathing, our ears cocked.

Then, there was the sound of a gun. Bang! Only one shot, like it had hit its mark. Angel started crying. Scared Clay had gone and shot Grandmommy, I cried along with Angel.

Aunt Bony jumped up and ran to the window but it was too dark out to see anything. Nothing we could do but wait. I closed my eyes and prayed, *Please God, let Clay be dead.*

After what seemed like hours, we heard footsteps. We still didn't know who was dead and who was alive. Finally, we heard voices, then Mama came in like nothing happened, Clay right behind her.

Aunt Bony untangled her long legs and stood tall. "Where's Mama? Edward?" she screamed.

"Everybody's all right," Mama said, "No thanks to you." Mama pointed to the door.

"Gee whiz, Betty," Aunt Bony said.

"Get."

Aunt Bony started towards the door, then turned and shook her fist at Clay. "You better not hurt the girls," she threatened.

"Get," Mama said again. Aunt Bony headed on out the door.

LuWanda M. Cheney

Clay sat down at the table and ran his hands through his hair. "I can't believe Bones accused me of something I wouldn't ever do," he whined. "Why'd I want to touch that bony thing when I got you? She's just a skinny kid."

"I know it," Mama said, pulling Clay close.

Early next morning, just as the pink sun peeked through the trees, Grandmommy and I went out to milk Bossy like we did every day. The bloated cow stared at us with dead eyes, her tongue hanging out her mouth. Purple. Swelled up. The sweet baby cow lay sprawled out next to its Mama, not moving.

"Hon," Grandmommy yelled, "The cow's been poisoned! Calf, too."

Didn't take me long to figure out who did it.

They all came running to see the dead cow. Clay got there first. "Guess Grandpa can't stop people from doing what they want," he whispered. "And Grandmommy's precious Jesus can't help either."

Now, I knew. Nobody could help me.

"**B**etty, you stay home today," Grandpa said. "Me and Edward will help Clay with the logging." Uncle Edward told us later that Clay told him to chase chain, but Grandpa said, "Naw, it's too dangerous. He's just a stupid kid. Let him drive the truck. *You* chase chain. I'll stand up in the truck and guide the logs." And that's the way it went, except Grandpa accidentally let the logs go and they piled up on top of Clay, causing him to be laid up in the hospital, hurt bad. Mama said he might die. I was praying he would. Most likely I wasn't the only one.

I'm pretty sure Mama was the only one praying for a miracle.

Two months had gone by. Mama came back from the hospital with a big grin on her face. "Clay is comin' home tomorrow," she said.

Grandmommy put her hand on Grandpa's arm. "Hon, we'd best be heading to Colorado. Matt wrote that he's getting out of the Marines. Roy's out of the Navy. They need your help getting their new construction company going."

"Still no word from Ralph?" Grandpa asked.

"Not yet."

As Grandmommy and Grandpa got ready to leave, Angel and I packed our little suitcases and ran to the car. Mama stood between the car and us, her hands on her hips. "You're not going anywhere," she said.

"Betty Lou, let us take the girls. In the name of Jesus."

"They're *my* girls. Clay misses the girls, and, after all these months, he's *finally* coming home. They've *got* to be here, you know. Clay *loves* the girls. He misses them."

"Betty Lou, you be careful. Don't you trust Clay with your girls."

Mama had the stubborn look on her face. "Goodbye," she said.

Grandpa started the car. "Noooo!" I screamed, as the car started down the road. "We want to go. Mama, please let us go. We want to go *home*."

Angel ran down the road after the car dragging her suitcase, her chubby little legs going fast as they could. The car out of sight, Angel threw herself down in the road, pounded her dimpled little fists into the gravel, kicked her legs and screamed, "Grandpaaa. Grandpaaa. Come back."

Mama sighed. "Go get her."

Angel lay face down in the middle of the road. "C'mon," I said. I wanted to take Angel and keep on going down the road to Grandpa's, but I was only six years old. I didn't know the way. "C'mon," I said again.

Angel's crying had changed from a howl to a high whiny hum. She sat up and looked at me with enormous watery eyes, mouth puckered up. "Clay's coming back. What if he shoots us?"

I patted her silky blonde hair. "If he tries to hurt you, I'll kill him," I promised.

---◆——◆---

It was autumn now, wet and raw. Days grew short. Nights were cold. Gaudy orange leaves clashed against blue sky. I was tramping through the red, orange, and yellow leaves, headed to the cabin. I burst in, anxious to get my hands on the lemon meringue pie Mama had promised me for after school. Mama didn't much like to cook but she was proud of her lemon meringue pie with its sweet-sour filling, the meringue peaks high, golden brown on the tips.

But there was no pie, only an empty plate. Then I heard the bed squeak. I whirled around and bumped into Clay. He had me cornered. I Scooted past him and ran out the door. Clay was right behind me. He grabbed me and threw me to the ground. He was on top of me. He was heavy. His checkered wool jacket was rough and smelled like sweat. He kissed me on the mouth. I turned my head. He mumbled in my ear. I could feel knuckles pressing into my thigh as he fumbled with the hard buttons on his jeans. His thing poked my leg, hurting me. One rough hand covered my mouth so the scream couldn't get out, the other hand pulled up my skirt and tore at my panties. I couldn't breathe. I felt hot breath on my face. His whiskers were scratchy. Mean yellow eyes told me he was gonna do something awful.

I heard the snarl at the same time I saw the flash of orange and black spring through the air and land with a thud on Clay's back. Lyptus's lips curled back. I saw her sharp teeth. Clay saw them, too. He rolled away from me and lay face down, his arms protecting his head. Lyptus tore at his jacket. I jumped up and ran to the cabin, Lyptus right behind me. Clay was on his feet now. He got to the door at the same time we did. Lyptus crouched down between Clay and me, showing her teeth and growling. Clay backed off.

Now Lyptus and I were inside the cabin. I locked the door.

Clay pounded on the door. "Open this damn door!" he screamed.

I hunkered down in the corner with Lyptus. She sat facing the door, ears up, hair on her back standing up. I sat with my arms around Lyptus, my fingers clutching her fur. She turned and licked my face. "Good dog. Good dog," I said over and over again.

Suddenly Clay appeared at the window. Lyptus ran to the window, laid back her ears and growled so mean the hair on the back of my neck stood on end. "Good dog," Clay said. "Let me in, darling. Daddy Clay didn't mean to scare you. Daddy loves you. I wouldn't hurt you. You believe me, don't you?" I didn't answer. Now Clay was pounding on the door with both fists. "Let me in, you stupid little shitass."

I was thinking, *I have to do something. I have to kill him.* I remembered Mama's gun. The shelf on the stove. The coffee can where Mama kept her gun. I pushed a chair up to the stove, took down the can and pried it open with a spoon handle.

Mama's gun was gone!

I shriveled down in the corner, closed my eyes and pretended I wasn't there.

——————————◆——————————

Mama was knocking on the door. "Let me in. What's going on here? Why is this door locked? What's that dog doing in the house?"

"Clay tried to do something bad. Lyptus didn't let him."

"What was he trying to do?"

"I don't know. Put his thing in me."

Mama marched outside to talk to Clay. I figured that was the end of him bothering me. *Thank you, Jesus.* I stood at the window and watched and listened. I was waiting for Mama to whop Clay upside the head and beat the tar out of him. I was hoping she'd shoot him.

"What happened?" Mama asked Clay.

Clay lied easily. It came natural. "She was playing with the dog and the damn stupid mutt knocked her down. I came running out the outhouse to help her and the barn door was open, and the mule fell out. That must be what scared her." Clay put a pitiful look on his face. "Damn, how could I be so careless? The poor little thing. I feel awful. You believe me, don't you?"

I held my breath.

"Well, sure I believe you, Honey."

Mama came back inside. "You made a mistake." She chewed on her lip. "Daddy Clay was trying to help you, you know."

"He was hurting me."

"Daddy Clay would never hurt his little girl."

"But he did."

Mama tossed her head and stuck her chin out. "You're wrong," she said. "Daddy Clay would *never* hurt his little girl."

———————◆—◆———————

Early next morning, before daybreak, I watched as Clay crept out of bed and tiptoed across the floor and out the door, being careful not to wake Mama. It was barely light when he came back, took the blue speckled coffee pot off the stove, and handed it to me. "You're big enough to do a few chores around here. Take this coffee pot down to the well and bring up some water."

The sun was just beginning to rise, the air still cold as night. I dressed quickly, grabbed the coffee pot, and skipped down the hill to the well, proud and happy to be big enough to do chores. I looked up at the handle that I had seen Mama turn many times. I reached up. I could not reach it. I climbed up and straddled the edge of the well. The stones were rough and cold. I grabbed the handle with my right hand and held it tightly. It was much harder to turn than I expected. I turned and turned and turned and the rope wound itself slowly around the pulley, raising the bucket inch by inch by inch. When the bucket was raised, I wrapped the rope around the spike so it wouldn't slip and unwind itself, lowering the bucket before I could get water.

I leaned out over the well to grab the bucket. I looked down into the well. The deep dark water looked almost black. I grabbed hold the bucket with both hands. It was heavy. I tightened my grip and, with considerable difficulty, managed to set the bucket on the edge of the well.

Now I reached for the ladle hanging from a nail and dipped it into the bucket. But the ladle did not slice through the water as I expected. It landed with a thunk. I peered into the bucket. Some wet thing was in the bucket, soggy gray fur plastered against its body. Mouth open. Dead eyes. Long tail, no longer bushy, folded against its back.

Squirrel was in the bucket.

He was dead!

Clay and Mama came running down the hill. Clay reached me before Mama did. He whispered, "That's what happens when you tell what you ain't supposed to tell."

Somebody was screaming and screaming and screaming. Maybe it was me.

At that moment the child I had been ceased to exist.

10

So far, I have told you how it all began. As disjointed memories of my past came to me, I pieced together the first six years of my life, and all that had happened to the child that I had been. I wrote it down in this book. And now I share these memories with you because, well, because I have to tell somebody.

I didn't know it at the time, and not for many years afterwards, but when I, at six-years old, was bombarded with more than I could endure, the child within me retreated to a safe dark place in my mind so that she wouldn't have to deal with the pain.

My mind had splintered and created separate and distinct personalities.

The Child had been traumatized. She endured horrendous assaults on both mind and body. She had been cut with a sharp knife and threatened with a gun. Her animal friends had been killed. Baby deer. Mama cow and her baby. Squirrel. When she found her best friend, Squirrel, dead in the bucket, her little mind splintered, shielding her from unbearable pain. At that moment, I became *The Other Child*. I knew nothing about the bad stuff. It was as if I just popped into existence.

The Protector appeared soon after, making her little hands into fists, doing her best to protect *us*. I switched from one to the other, unaware of the others.

———————————————

Sidran Institute explains this dissociative process best:

> When faced with overwhelming traumatic situations from which there is no physical escape, a child may resort to "going away" in his or her head. Children typically use this ability as an extremely effective defense against acute physical and emotional pain, or anxious anticipation of that pain. By this dissociative process, thoughts, feelings, memories and perceptions of the traumatic experiences can be separated off psychologically, allowing the child to function as if the trauma had not occurred.
>
> Dissociative Disorders are often referred to as highly creative survival technique because they allow individuals enduring "hopeless" circumstances to preserve some areas of healthy functioning. Over time, however, for a child who has been repeatedly physically and sexually assaulted, defensive dissociative escape is so effective, children who are very practiced at it may automatically use it whenever they feel threatened or anxious- even if the anxiety-producing situation is not extreme or abusive.
>
> Repeated dissociation may result in a series of separate entities, or mental states, which may become the internal "personality states" of a DID system. Changing between these states of consciousness is often described as "switching."

©Reprinted with permission from Sidran Institute.

And now you know more about the characters, at this point, than they know about themselves. Now I will tell you what happened next:

—————————— ✦ —————— ✦ ——————————

The Other Child:

...I woke up in an unfamiliar place, wondering, *Where am I? Who are these people? And why aren't they surprised to see me?* There was a little girl in bed with me. She had a sweet, dimpled face, pink cheeks, fine blonde hair and large hazel eyes. She smiled. I thought maybe I knew her. "Who are you?" I whispered.

"Call me Angel."

"Who's that?" I asked, pointing to the woman at the stove.

She giggled. "It's Mama."

There was a man sitting at the table. He grinned at me. "Him?" I nodded in the man's direction.

"It's Daddy Clay, silly."

As far as I could tell, this was my own family, but I didn't know them. I wondered where I had been and how long I had been gone.

"Get ready," the woman said. I had no idea what she was talking about.

"Time to get dressed for school," Angel said, pointing at the clothes laid out on the bed. I was amazed that the clothes were just my size. I dressed and followed Angel to the table. "Good morning, Mother. Good morning, Father," I said. They smiled at me, and I smiled back, pleased to discover I had such a perfect family. We were halfway through breakfast when I first heard the child cry. The cries were muffled, yet very near. I got up and peered into the shadowy corner behind the stove. I looked under the bed and pulled back the patchwork quilt.

"What are you looking for?" Mother asked.

"Somebody's crying. Don't you hear her?" Mother shook her head like she didn't know what I was talking about.

I thought I saw a shadow in the far corner, but when I got close I saw it was only a large bag of potatoes. I looked under the table. Mother watched me with an odd look on her face. I wondered, *Does she know more than she lets on?* I knew there was another little girl hiding somewhere. I could hear her sobbing pitifully somewhere in the shadows.

"Time to go," Mother said.

I got on the yellow bus like Angel told me. I had no idea where I was going. "Where am I supposed to go?" I asked the curly-headed girl who sat next to me on the bus.

"Miss Schauble's classroom, same as always," she said, taking my hand and leading me down the hall. I would have sworn I had never been there before. The curly-headed girl sat down at a desk. There were maybe thirty desks lined up in rows. They all looked the same to me. I wondered, *Where am I supposed to sit?* I waited until everyone else sat down, and then sat in the one remaining seat.

Miss Schauble did not look familiar, but I could see right away that she had escaped from Hell. She was a demon who came to school disguised as a first-grade teacher. She, of course, enforced all the rules. She did it for fun. No running in the halls. No talking in class. And especially no chewing gum. If Miss Schauble caught you chewing gum she screamed, "Gum!" Then she made you take the gum out of your mouth and stick it on your nose.

Miss Schauble left the room, and a handful of us dared to talk out loud. Without raising our hands. Without permission. When she came back, a boy called Michael tattled, "Teacher, they was talking." I was thinking, *Michael was talking the most.*

"Who was talking?" Miss Schauble demanded to know.

Michael pointed to two other girls, a boy and me.

"Were you talking while I was gone?"

The girls lowered their eyes and nodded. The boy and I said, "No." Miss Schauble told the guilty girls to go to the front of the room, took a ruler from the desk drawer and smacked it against the palm of her hand in a threatening manner. She gave the boy and me one last chance. "Were you talking while I was out of the room?" The boy admitted he had been talking. He took his place in front of the room, while Miss Schauble led the class, rubbing one forefinger across the other and chanting, "Shame, shame on you-oo, Shame, shame on you-oo."

Miss Schauble glared at me with cold eyes. "Hold out your hands." The ruler came down hard. Miss Schauble's eyes bulged. Her face was red. Between clenched teeth she asked again, "Did you talk?"

"No," I lied. I did it 'cause I thought she was stupid.

The ruler landed again. "Did you talk?"

"No."

Miss Schauble turned the ruler on its side and whacked me across the back of my hands. The sharp metal edge drew a thin line of blood straight across both hands. And now I felt a new emotion. Like some kind of poison, my anger seemed to ferment, bubble up and spill out, filling me with rage. I closed my eyes and disappeared...

———————————◆—◆———————————

The Protector:
...My body stiff, my eyes narrow, I made my hands into fists. I was thinking, *I can protect myself. Nobody can make me do what I don't want to do. I won't let a dimwit like Miss Schauble shame me. Who does she think she's talking to?*

Miss Schauble said, "Stay in for recess." "No lunch." And when she collected my arithmetic paper, one plucked eyebrow shot up. "This paper's dirty," she said gleefully. "Do it over."

I made no move to take the paper back. Miss Schauble glared at me. I pursed my lips and glared back. Miss Schauble repeated, "This paper's dirty. Do it over."

"I *like* blood on my papers," I said defiantly.

At a quarter past two I raised my hand. I hadn't been allowed to leave my desk all day.

Miss Schauble said, "No, you may not go to the bathroom."

I raised my hand three more times. Miss Schauble wouldn't call me. I squeezed my legs together. It didn't help. Warm pee ran down my leg, making a yellow puddle under my chair. Michael snickered and pointed. I put my head down and pretended to sleep. I stayed like that until the dismissal bell rang.

After the other children had gone, Miss Schauble handed me a rag. "Mop it up."

The pee stung my cuts. I stuck out my chin and made my hands into fists. *Nobody can make me do what I don't want to do.* Between clenched teeth I said, "I *like* to mop up pee. I *always* ask Mother, 'Please, please, let me mop up my little sister's pee.'"

--- ◆ --- ◆ ---

The Other Child
"Angel," I asked, "Do we have a dog named Spot?"

"No, silly. We have a dog named Lyptus. She didn't come home. She didn't eat her dinner."

"I'll find her." It was Saturday, and Angel said there was no school, so I went looking for the lost dog, calling, "Lyptus. Lyptus." My cries were lost in the wind.

I searched until dark, then went to bed without eating.

Next morning, I set out early, and traveled a path through the woods, keeping one eye out for the dog and the other eye out for danger. It was a sunny day and that made for shadows in the woods. Every now and then I would stop and stare into shadowy places thinking I had seen a dog, and more than once I called out, "Lyptus" only to find I had called out to a log, or a stump.

The wind began to blow, rustling the leaves in the trees. I tip-toed down the path, head up, as if expecting to see something in the trees, and when I saw a squirrel's nest high up in a large old pine tree, I heard a little girl sobbing.

When I saw the thing in the path, not moving, I did not want to know what it was. I threw myself down on the ground and crawled inside myself...

The Child:
...I found Lyptus with a bullet hole in her head. Blood. So much blood. I tried to carry her home but could not budge the cold, hard lifeless thing.

The sun dipped down behind the trees. I shivered and headed back to the cabin.

Clay and Mama were sitting at the table drinking whiskey. I made up my mind to tell, no matter what Clay did to me. I took a deep breath. "Mama," I said, "I found Lyptus in the woods. She's dead."

"A tree fell on her and killed her," Clay was quick to explain.

"Lyptus was killed by a bullet."

"I had to shoot her so she wouldn't suffer."

"What about me suffering?" I said, remembering a verse from the Bible. "I know Jesus said, 'suffer the little children' but didn't I already suffer enough?"

Mama looked at me like she didn't know me.

I walked over to my bed and threw the shell quilt, the one that used to be magic, on the floor, climbed into bed and covered my head with my pillow. Grandpa had been my last hope to stop Clay. He couldn't do it. I had no hope left. I was afraid Clay would kill everything I loved. I cried for Lyptus, Squirrel, the calf and mama cow, the baby deer and finally for myself. I cried until my eyes were red and swollen. I sank deeper and deeper into the soft black place until my cries became muffled and then faded away...

The Other Child:

...Oddly, I found myself back at the cabin. I went inside and stepped into the shadows beyond the light of the kerosene lantern and stood listening to the crying of the child who was lost somewhere in the darkness. I peered into the dark. I reached out my arms. There was no one there. I closed my eyes and escaped to the black place...

...I woke feeling sad, my face wet with tears I hadn't cried. And I didn't know why.

Angel stared at me, her forehead puckered. "You're the other one, aren't you?" she whispered.

I nodded, relived that somebody knew. Mother, Father, Miss Schauble, the kids at school, they all had me confused with another little girl, the child I wanted to find, the one I heard crying in the shadows. They didn't know I was The Other Child. They didn't know me. I didn't even know who I was. I had just popped into existence, and no one acknowledged me, as if I didn't exist. If it hadn't been for Angel, things would've been a lot worse. She was only four, yet she knew. She knew, and she looked after me, and told me what I didn't know, "Don't call her 'Mother'. You got that outta your schoolbook. Say 'Mama,' And don't say 'Father'. His name is 'Daddy Clay'. And we don't got a dog named 'Spot'."[6]

––––––––––––––––––

By the time the first snow fell, Clay had raped the land and destroyed the green, green woods. There were no trees left, they had all been killed. The forest was dead. Nothing but dead stumps as far as the eye could see. The birds had gone. And the deer. Clay had defiled the forest, destroying everything in his path.

Mama loaded the last of our belongings into the Chevy. "Let's go. Get in the car."

"What about Kitty."

––––––––––––––––––

6. Dick, Jane, Mother, Father and Spot were characters in a series of books written by William S. Gray that taught children to read..

"The horse isn't going with us."

I didn't ask why.

I curled up inside myself where it was black and warm and soft as velvet...

11

Port Gamble, Washington 1947

The Other Child:

... A *great black cloud of sadness rose up and landed on me like a swarm of locusts. Even when we moved, crossing on the ferry, past the winking, blinking lighthouse that kept the boats from banging into the rocks, The Sadness was there. A seagull followed the ferry. I was thinking, I wish I could fly. The Sadness leapt up out of the shadows and sat on my shoulders, weighing me down.*

We moved into a gray house. Everybody in Port Gamble lived in gray houses. Gray houses all in a row on both sides of the street, same as on the next street and the next. The only way I could tell our house from the others was to start at the fire hydrant, then count one, two, three, four, *five*. That was our house. It wasn't *really* our house. One man owned all the houses, the sawmill where Clay worked, the store and the bar. I'm not sure if he owned the church or not. He let us live in one of his houses. Clay said it was because he worked for him. Mama said it was because we gave him too much rent.

Everything there was gray. Gray houses marching down to gray sand. Gray sky. Gray mist rising from a cold pewter sea. Sometimes a thick fog covered the dunes. Lighthouse standing guard. The sad sound of a foghorn crying out.

There were some children there, but I didn't know them. They were like gray shadows at dusk. Shadows. Gray sky. Fog. And *The Sadness*.

At the sawmill where Clay worked was a big round saw called a buzz saw on account of the sound it made. Sometimes the men called it a gash saw 'cause it could rip through wood. Or a man. Mama worried about that saw. There was no way to lock it. It started up whenever you put the electricity on. Sure enough, one day Clay was sharpening the saw and Big Red turned on the electricity The saw started up and Clay came home with his hand bandaged. That meant Mama had to go back to work. Maybe she was playing piano in the bar. I can't say for sure. I do know she worked nights. "I'll take care of the girls," Clay promised. "Don't worry."

"When you coming home, Mama?"

"Don't worry about it. You just do what Daddy Clay tells you. I'll be along."

Clay's not my daddy. My real daddy is coming back.

———————————————◆—————————◆———————————

The Child:

I woke from a sound sleep too scared to move. I heard the wind rustling in the tall, dry reeds along the shore. The wind was blowing against the window, seeping in through cracks. I shivered. November had blown in on frigid wind. Now the frost-tipped silver sand lay frozen. The black maples, without leaves, like huge many-fingered hands reached up through frozen ground and pointed towards the pewter sea that gleamed faintly, like an aged mirror.

I heard the foghorn warning about danger. Angel was asleep. She was safe.

The room was dark. Clay's shadow was standing in the door. He whispered my name. I pretended to sleep. *God, please save me. In the name of Jesus. Amen.* I guess God didn't hear because Clay came nearer, belt hanging like a snake off his skinny, hairy arm. He hissed, "When I call, you better come running." The belt whistled through the air and landed, leaving a hot stinging welt on my thigh. "Why didn't you come when I called you?" Clay whined. "You hurt my feelings when you don't come when I need you. Daddy Clay loves you, darling. We're gonna have a little snack. Just you and me. You're big enough to stay up late. We can have lots of fun."

"I get sleepy if I stay up too late."

"If you don't want to stay up late to have treats, maybe Angel Puss does."

"Angel's sleeping."

"If you don't want to stay up with Daddy Clay, I can wake up Angel."

Please God. Don't let Clay touch Angel. In the name of Jesus...

The Protector:
...I had to protect Angel. "I want snacks," I said. Clay started towards Angel's bed. "I want snacks," I said louder. "Let Angel sleep."

Clay slammed his fist down on Angel's bed. "Wake up, Angel Puss," he said. "It's time for a snack." *Mama's peanut butter cookies don't taste good. Milk tastes bad. Tears taste like salt.*

"Take off your clothes," Clay said. "It's time for bed."

Angel said, "But we already got our jamas on."

"They're dirty. Your Mama forgot to wash 'em. You'll have to sleep with me. You'll be cold without your jamas." Clay reached out and touched Angel's bottom. When we got into bed, I got in the middle so he wouldn't touch Angel, then he touched me. I pretended to sleep while Clay touched himself and wiggled the bed, then he got a wash rag and wiped slimy stuff off the bed.

"What on earth?" Mama said, surprised to find us naked in bed with Clay.

"I couldn't find their pajamas," Clay whined. "They were cold. They wanted to sleep with me."

"They're right here in the drawer," Mama said, tossing our jamas to the floor. I fetched them, handed Angel's to her and slipped into mine quick as could be.

"Just like a man," Mama muttered under her breath, "Can't find nuthin'. Couldn't find 'em if they was stuck on the end of your nose."

I pulled back the covers so Mama would see the wet spot. Mama wrinkled her nose like she was disgusted, grabbed my arm and shook me. "Are you turning into a baby to start wetting the bed? And how come you're too scared to sleep in your own bed?"

"I don't wet the bed. Neither does Angel."

Clay came up behind me and pressed his thumbs into my shoulders. His fingers dug in under my collarbone, his thumbs pressing into my shoulder blades. "Don't you fib," he said. "You'll get a licking."

I tightened up my body, pressed my lips tightly together and made my hands into fists. *Nobody can make me do what I don't want to do.* "I'm not fibbing," I yelled. "*You* got the bed wet."

Clay drug me into the bathroom, took off his belt, wrapped one end around his hand, pulled my jamas down, lay me across his lap, caressed my bare bottom, then whipped me. The belt whistled through the air and landed again and again. I screamed each time it landed. Mama stood outside the door. I knew she could hear me scream. I wondered, *How come Mama doesn't make him stop?*

Finally, after a very long time, Mama said, "That's enough.". Mama wasn't scared of Clay. She could have made him stop sooner. She must've figured I had it coming. Now she sunk her fingernails into my arm. "Did you think you'd get away with fibbing? Did you think I'd really believe Clay wet the bed?"

I wanted to tell Mama what happened, but I didn't know how. And Clay was standing in the doorway, his belt still wrapped around his hand. I knew all about what Clay had done. *The Other Child*—she didn't know what was going on. And *The Child*, she couldn't do anything to stop Clay. I heard her crying in the dark. I was bigger. It was up to me.

I knew I'd have to kill Clay to stop him.

The Protector:

When Mama got out the butcher knife and whacked up a chicken for supper, I watched with particular interest. It was the knife that had my attention. Grandpa had made the knife, cut it from a piece of steel, hammered it and sharpened it. It was razor-sharp.

Now I knew *how* I'd kill Clay.

That night after Mama and Clay fell asleep, I sneaked down into the kitchen. The moon was near full, so I stayed in the shadows, close to the wall, just in case they woke up. I rummaged through the drawers until I found the knife. It was heavy but not too heavy for me. I was big. I was seven. I held the knife in my right hand and made stabbing motions in the air. The burnished steel edge shone in the moonlight like a magic sword. When my arm got tired, I hid the knife under the stairs, feeling good inside, knowing I could protect Angel if I had to. I'd stick the knife into Clay's heart, or I'd slice off his head and send it rolling down the stairs, and if Mama noticed it, and asked what it was doing there, I'd say, "I don't know."

I smiled to myself, a big, full-toothed smile, and wondered if I'd have to use the knife.

The Other Child:

Something incomprehensible had happened. I knew it was something terrible, but the details were locked away in *The Child's* mind. I sat, propped up on the sofa, lost in a black empty place. Clay sat on the armchair, trying to look pitiful. Angel was shaking Christmas presents, trying to figure out what they were. "What do you think you got?" she asked. "What do you hope it is?"

"It don't matter to me."

Mama said we could open our presents, even though it was three days before Christmas. Angel ripped open the largest box. An electric stove. She handed me a package, but I didn't feel like opening it.

Clay jumped up and presented Mama with a package not much bigger than a deck of cards. Mama slowly untied the crimson ribbon, carefully removed the silvery paper, folded it and put it in her pocket. She lifted the top, peeked inside and giggled.

"Do you like it?" Clay asked.

Mama grinned. She slid the gold watch up over her left hand and held it at arm's length so we could admire it.

"Don't go," Clay pleaded.

"I have to."

"You're right. I don't deserve you."

"Damn right."

Clay sat, with his head in his hands. "I've lost my little family. It's my own fault. How can I go on without you?"

"You should've thought of that."

"I'll change. You'll see. I'll prove it to you. Go on. Get as far away from me as you can. I'm no good. I'm a monster. But I'll change. You'll see."

"I'll call a cab."

"Let me drive you to the train."

"That won't be necessary."

"It's the least I can do."

12

Trinidad, Colorado 1947

The Other Child:

The Sadness followed me everywhere now, crouching down, waiting for a chance to jump on my back. Even as the train clickety clacked its way to Grandpa's, The Sadness was there. I pretended to read my book, an early Christmas present, so Mama wouldn't be sad. I was thinking, *I'm too old for Christmas.*

It was dark when the 8:15 pulled into Trinidad. Mama pulled Angel's cap down over her ears, handed me my coat and slipped into hers. The white-haired, brown-skinned conductor reached up to help Mama down out the train. She giggled when he offered his hand.

Mama pointed. "There's your Uncle Matt. I told you he was tall, dark and handsome." He wasn't that tall; it just seemed that way to Mama because she was all hunkered over. Seemed like she had shrunk over the past few days.

Uncle Matt led us to a navy Pontiac, carrying our cardboard boxes tied with string, and Mama's familiar tan suitcase. "You all right?"

"You know me. I'm tough."

"How about her?" Uncle Matt jerked his head in my direction.

"Well as can be expected, I guess."

"Clay?"

"Who cares?" Mama lit a cigarette, took a drag and burst into tears.

Angel had fallen asleep in the car, her eyes shut tight as a newborn kitten. Mama handed her over to a pewter-haired lady who smelled like lavender. I didn't know her.

"Where's Grandpa's hug?" The man held out his arms. I turned away. He peered at me from beneath black, bushy eyebrows with sad brown eyes. A tear rolled slowly down his cheek. He wiped it off with the cuff of his sleeve. "Grandpa doesn't get a hug?" I shook my head.

The one called Grandpa pulled out a little bed from beneath a bigger bed. "Remember the bed Grandpa made for you? And your magic quilt?" The bed did not look familiar. But after while I remembered the quilt. When I was little, I used to think the shells were magic. I was big now. I was seven. I climbed into bed and snuggled up to the pillow fish with blue button eyes and patted his purple velvet tail.

A tall barefoot girl brought me an orange and white striped kitty. "You little skunk, here's a little tiger to keep you warm," she said in a slow deep voice. As she walked away, I heard her say, "Poor little thing."

I yelled, "I'm *not* a poor little thing."

"Not you, honey," Mama lied, "Aunt Bony was talking about that poor skinny little kitty." I knew she meant me. I curled up in a ball, hugged the tiger kitty and rocked myself to sleep.

It was just before dawn when I woke. The back of my neck prickled. I was not alone. I could hear a child sobbing. The cries were muffled, yet close by, as if she were hiding in some dark place. I thought she might be hiding in the bed. I pulled back the covers. Angel was sound asleep. There was no one else. Who was crying? I knew it must be the child I thought we had left behind.

I searched under the bed, behind the door and in the closet. The cries were louder now. The child was very near. Now I heard noises coming from outside my bedroom. Stepping into the hall, I headed towards the sound, tiptoeing down the hall. There was a light coming from the room at the end of the hall. I crept towards the light, listening. There was no other sound now except for the sobbing child. When I reached the door, I slipped inside. Grandmommy was standing at the stove. I stood in the shadows and watched as she crumbled corn bread and mixed it with chopped onion, celery and sage, then stuffed the biggest turkey I ever saw. There was no sign of the child. Grandmommy slid the turkey into the oven and turned to face me. "Well now," she said, "What are you doing up at this hour?"

"I heard somebody crying,"

"Who? Who was crying?"

"It's the child. She's hiding and I can't find her."

Grandmommy took my hand and led me through the house, opening doors, pulling out drawers, even kneeling down to look under beds. "There. You see, there's no one."

"But I heard her crying."

Grandmommy led me back to bed. "Lord, have mercy."

I lay in bed, staring into the dark, trying to stay awake in case the child came back.

The next day, after breakfast, I sat in the corner thinking about the child I heard crying in the night and trying to sort out all the people. I sat watching and listening to what they said about each other. "Bones still lives at home," they said. "She's twenty, just eight months short of being able to drink legally." "Bones is tall," they said, "Legs like a giraffe, long and always in the way, and she still wears blue jeans." "Wonder if she'll ever change."

"Ethel's expecting. Again." "You'd think she'd learn," they said. "Roy Junior so quiet since the orphanage. Her, with her migraines, spending half her life lying in bed in a darkened room." "I wonder what Roy sees in her."

While the women gossiped, the men climbed into Uncle Roy's truck, went into the woods and came home with the biggest Christmas tree I'd ever seen. The gigantic tree was to go in the front room opposite the bay window. According to Grandpa's ruler, the ceilings were four yardsticks high, the tree measured five. Even after Grandpa cut two feet off the top and a foot off the trunk, they couldn't get the tree through the door.

The women busied themselves in the kitchen, pretending not to notice. Aunt Bony stationed herself at the window and amused them with reports of the progress, or lack of it.

Grandpa wrapped rope round and round, pulling the branches tight to the trunk. Uncle Roy took the door off the hinges. They tried again, this time scratching the doorframe and chipping the paint. They still could not get the tree in the door.

During dinner, no one mentioned the tree.

After we ate, my uncles removed the bay window as if it were the most natural thing in the world, leaving a hole in the wall through which elephants could walk, two by two. They brought the tree in through the hole. The magnificent spruce, once in place, stretched twelve feet to the ceiling. Grandpa, standing on a ladder, hung an angel at the top, then Grandmommy wasted no time in decorating it with shimmering silver icicles, fancy ornaments, and silver cones filled with hard candies.

When Grandmommy had gone, I walked around the wonderful tree, admiring the fancy decorations, and breathing in the fragrance of the forest. It was then that I noticed a tiny squirrel hanging precariously from a branch just over my head. I sucked in air and stared at the squirrel. He looked at me with sad black eyes. My head felt like somebody had stretched a thick rubber band over my forehead and snapped it across the back of my head. I reached up and took the squirrel off the tree and put it in my pocket where it would be safe, then crawled under and stood up behind the tree next to The Sadness. I didn't want anybody to look at me, thinking they knew who I was when they did not. They didn't know me. They all thought I was somebody else. Nobody cared about the little girl I had replaced. Nobody cared about the child who cried alone. The Sadness reached down inside my stomach and squeezed.

In my secret hiding place, I watched as more people arrived. Each added presents to the pile until there were a jillion presents beneath the tree. They all seemed to be moving in slow motion and when their mouths moved, they sounded like bees buzzing inside an upside-down glass. I didn't know any of them, but they were my *relations*. Mama said so.

Every now and then Grandmommy stopped to look out the window. Seeing no one, she sighed, mumbled to Jesus and set the table with an extra place.

"Who's the extra place for?" Angel asked.

Aunt Bony answered, "Your Uncle Ralph went off to the war. We haven't heard from him since. She sets a place for him at every meal."

Now Aunt Bony looked out the window. "Mama, Edward's home! Gee whiz, he has on his uniform. Look!"

Grandmommy wiped her hands on her apron and flung the door open wide. "Praise the Lord!"

The one called Edward was dressed like a Marine, looking like he should be on a poster with Uncle Sam. He hugged Grandmommy, then swooped up Angel, put her on his shoulders and carried her piggyback, giggling, to find Grandpa.

The one called Alberta arrived next, wearing black with pink polka dots. High heels. Pearls. Smiling lips painted red. She leaned on the arm of her new husband- the third, I think, a gaunt gangly man with a plain face and sharply angled lines around his mouth and eyes. His big hands hung awkwardly at his side. At six foot two, he stood exactly one foot taller than Alberta.

Angel ran squealing, "Aunt Alberta, did you bring me a present?"

Aunt Alberta fussed over Angel's blonde hair. "Where's Lucinda?"

"Lucinda," Mama called. Lucinda– that's what they called me. The name sounded odd. They all called me that, but I was somebody else. And I wondered, *What happened to the child they think is me? Where is she?*

It was Christmas morning. Angel took my hand and drug me to the window seat in the parlor to look at snow so white it hurt your eyes. The wind came down off the mountain, whistled at the windows and howled at the door. Frigid wind rushed in and wrapped itself around our ankles. Grandpa came in the door, carrying an armload of firewood, and dropped down on one knee in front of the fireplace. Using his knife, he shaved slivers off dry kindling wood, fiddled with the firewood and struck a match. The flame flickered and burst into flame. The fire crackled and danced. "That's a fine fire to keep you warm."

Aunt Bony brought a quilt and draped it over our shoulders. "Gee whiz, you little skunks, it's a white Christmas."

Aunt Alberta brought hot chocolate and a polka dot dress for my doll.

Angel climbed up next to me. She had gone blurry on me. "Want to play dolls?" She sounded muffled and far away. I shook my head. She put her arms around my neck, kissed my cheek and patted me on the head. I sat in the bay window watching the snow fall silently, making everything fresh and new until I was the only dirty thing left.

From the window I watched a yellow taxi pull to the curb. A sailor climbed out. The driver got out, too, opened the trunk and set two duffel bags on the sidewalk. He stood straight and saluted the sailor. The sailor saluted back before he picked up his gear.

Aunt Bony peeked out the window. "Mamma, It's Ralph!"

"Hallelujah!" Grandmommy ran slowly out the door and threw her arms around the sailor. "Praise God!" Her voice sounded quiet-like and far away.

Aunt Alberta rushed to the window. "Oh, my gosh. It really is Ralph!" She was jumping up and down and pointing out the window.

The odd thing was that they all moved in slow motion.

"Well, I'll be damned," Aunt Bony said. "He's got a woman with him. She's wearing a mink stole and a hat with a veil. Wonder who she thinks she is."

Aunt Alberta craned her neck to get a better look at the woman Uncle Ralph brought home. "Hmm, she's pretty but she sure is thin. And pale. Betty, come look."

Mama squished me against the window, trying to get a good look. "I've seen better," she said, unimpressed by the highfaluting lady. "She's *very, very* pale, you know, and *very, very* thin. Looks like death warmed over. And I doubt that's mink. Probably rabbit. Or *cat*."

Through the window I watched Grandmommy hug Uncle Ralph for a long, long time, then she straightened up and wiped tears from her eyes. "Y'all got here just in the nick of time," she said, her voice kind of scratchy. "Supper's on the table."

Now Grandpa hurried outside and took Uncle Ralph's hand in his, then dropped it and threw his arms around his son. Meanwhile, my other uncles heard the ruckus and ran outside to greet Uncle Ralph and the pretty woman he had brought home. Now they all came inside the house, their noses red, their hair white with snow.

Uncle Ralph escorted the pale, thin woman into the dining room. White damask covered the eighteen-foot table. Grandmommy set another blue willow place setting., making twenty-one settings. Grandpa lit six flickering beeswax candles. Bowls were heaped high with mashed potatoes, candied yams, green beans sprinkled with crisp bacon, boiled turnips and spiced crab apples. On the sideboard set the golden-brown turkey and a glazed ham studded with cloves.

I crawled under the sideboard.

Mama said, "Get to the table."

I shook my head. "I'm not hungry."

"Get to the table. Now." Mama stamped her foot and glared at me. I knew I'd better do what she said. I took my place at the table and sat, with the others, staring at the pretty woman.

Uncle Ralph cleared his throat. "This is Helen. My wife."

Mama rolled her eyes. At first nobody said anything, then they all talked at once.

"So, this is why we didn't hear from you." Uncle Matt grinned at the woman.

"I was on ship," Uncle Ralph said, "then stationed in Europe. Didn't you get my letters?"

"Not yet," Grandmommy said. "Helen, do you want dark meat, or light?"

————————◆━━━◆————————

"A fine Christmas they said. "The turkey moist, the cornbread stuffing seasoned just right." It was a Christmas to remember and one by which all future Christmas's would be measured.

Christmas over, Angel grabbed my hand. "C'mon. Let's put our dolls to sleep in their new beds."

The doll beds had feather stuffed mattresses and pillows. Sheets. Patchwork quilts. "Where'd they come from?" I asked.

"We got 'em from Santa Claus? Remember?" I racked my brain. It was no use. I couldn't remember. Angel patted me on the head and handed me a tiny nightgown trimmed in lace. "Let's play dolls."

"It's bedtime, Elizabeth," I said to my doll.

I was thinking, *Maybe I'm not too old for Christmas.*

13

In 1948 I was eight and Angel six. That was the summer the piss ants got into Grandmommy's kitchen. You'd have thought the world was coming to an end the way Grandmommy carried on.

Everybody had their own idea how to get rid of the ants. Uncle Roy spread thick sticky molasses on strips of paper and captured quite a few that way. Grandpa crushed them up and soaked them in water, then dripped the water all around the house so the ants would know this wasn't the place to be. But I thought Roy Junior had the best idea. He glued dead ants to toothpick crosses and placed them all around the property to warn the ants to stay away. He was eleven then and didn't have much to do with us girls, but he did let me help make the crosses. I'm not sure which plan worked but I do know the ants left and never came back.

On the 4th of July the whole family piled into the back of Uncle Roy's truck and drove thirty miles, then took a sharp left down the muddy brown road into Devil's Canyon. The sun was high in the sky. And hot. But it was cool in the shade under the trees and the river was cold. Mama dipped her hand into the river and splashed her face. "Whew, it's a scorcher."

"Yep," Grandpa said, as he put a watermelon in the river to cool.

Grandmommy dropped chunks of beef into a brown paper bag with seasoned flour, shook the bag until the meat was coated and browned it in hot fat. She added onion and garlic, then potatoes, carrots and rutabagas. Finally, she tossed in a little cheesecloth bundle, which held good smelling herbs from Grandpa's garden.

Angel ran off to play with my cousins in the river, splashing and laughing.

I walked along the river a piece, took off my shoes and waded downstream. That's when I saw the man in a red and black checkered jacket. My heart went whump whump whump. The man stepped into the stream, pretending to fish. He grinned.

I wanted to run but my feet wouldn't move. I got down on my stomach and hid, face down in the water where everything was green. I could see smooth green rocks and fuzzy green plants growing under the water. A quick green fish swam by. Face down in a watery fairy land, I hid from the man in the checkered shirt, watching and waiting for fairies, fairies like the ones in *The Water Babies*, fairies who could make you clean like they did the grimy chimney sweep. I waited and watched the sunbeams reflecting on the water. The water danced all around little green ferns. The ferns swayed in the water, making ferny shadows on the rocks. The sun shone down on the water and the mica in the stream shone like diamonds. I wanted to stay there forever.

I stayed face down in the water a long time.

Next thing I knew, Uncle Matt was pushing on my chest, and I was puking up river water.

"She almost drowned," they said, "Why was she scared of the fisherman? What was she doing? Was she trying to kill herself?"

The following year Aunt Bony married Glen. Uncle Matt convinced Aunt Bony she should have only blondes in her wedding party, so she'd stand out. "Ain't it a shame," they said, "Matt finagling to get next to that blonde hussy with the twins. Can't her husband see what's going on?"

Skinny blue-eyed yellow-haired twins walked down the aisle wearing long pink dresses and tossing rose petals in the aisle. I wished I was blonde and pretty so I could walk down the aisle in a long pink dress. The Sadness sat on my shoulders and chanted in my ear, "You're ugly, ugly, ugly." I reached up and wiped tears from my eyes.

Grandmommy said, "Do I see a green-eyed monster sitting beside me?"

"No, the smelly flowers the twins are throwing in the aisle make my eyes water."

After the wedding, I took a bath and scrubbed until I was red, but I never did get clean and pretty like other girls. No matter how hard I scrubbed, I was still dirty.

I knew I needed to be baptized in water. John the Baptist said so. Two weeks later, I waded out into the river, wearing a long white robe. The preacher prayed, "Lord, accept this child of God. In the name of Jesus. Amen." The preacher bent me over backwards in the water, under the water. Down, down, down into the water. I was falling, falling, falling down into the water. I was hoping it would make me clean.

The choir, dressed in purple robes, stood at the riverbank and sang gospel. The words poured over me, telling me I was good as anybody and just as clean.

I believed it. For a little while.

Mama took off right after the wedding. I was ten. Angel was eight. Mama was twenty-eight, too young to be tied down with two kids. Grandpa, Grandmommy, Angel and I headed back to Oregon. The war over, money wasn't so hard to come by so Grandpa built a new house. When he tore down the old house, I carried on something terrible. "Why is she so upset?" they said, "the house was about to fall down." They didn't understand. 412 West A was the only place where I had ever felt safe.

The new house had electricity, hard wood floors and a bathroom. Angel and I had our own room's now. Grandpa still had his garden and the walnut tree on account of he built the new house on the same piece of land.

I sat in the sunken garden reading, the sun warm against my back. Angel came and sat down beside me. "Where do you think Mama is?" she asked.

I shrugged. "No telling."

"Uncle Matt says he heard she's playing piano with a big band."

The heavy perfume of lilacs and roses filled the air. I breathed deeply, taking in the wonderful smells. Out of the corner of my eye, I caught a glimpse of a fairy fluttering nearby, its see-through wings golden, its dress iridescent greens and blues. She wanted me to follow her to the fairy camp. I climbed up on the stone wall, flapped my arms like wings and crash-landed in Grandpa's gourds.

Angel looked at me in a peculiar way. "You're weird," she said and walked away.

I twirled round and round in the sunken garden, my arms straight out to the side. I twirled faster and faster, like a spinning top, making myself dizzy. I staggered and fell face down on the lawn. That's when I found the fairy house tucked under the lilac bush. The size of a shoebox, it was painted green inside and out and carpeted with moss soft as velvet. Lace covered the windows. Tiny moss-covered logs became benches. A hollowed-out gourd stuffed with cotton made a fine bed, a Borage leaf a fuzzy, fragrant blanket. A tiny log stood on end, a slice of tree branch nailed to the top to make a table. On the table, a fat juicy blackberry on a round Nasturtium leaf, water in an acorn cup and a sliver of kindling, sharp like a knife, in case the fairies needed to cut the berry. Or kill a bad man.

Inside were clothespin dolls with silky floss hair, sheer green dresses, and wings made of seeds from oak trees. They wore hats of Foxglove blossoms turned upside down. I showed the dolls to Grandmommy. She said, "They're your fairies. I gave them to you for the fairy house you made."

"But I didn't make it. I found it on the lawn."

As I walked away, I heard Grandpa say, "Hon, Lucinda's a strange child. Can't remember a dad-burned thing."

"Lord, have mercy."

I was walking towards the house when I heard the muffled cry. She was back, the child I thought had been left behind. No matter what they said, I knew there was another little girl. People often mistook me for her. I had long ceased trying to explain that she and I were not the same. I didn't know her; we had never been in the same place at the same time, yet whenever I thought of her, or heard her cry, The Sadness reached out and wrapped long, bony fingers around my body and squeezed until I could hardly breathe. Somehow, I had taken her place and she had gone into hiding, and I knew it was my fault that she was gone. I walked faster. I wanted to find her. I needed to know what had happened to her, and why she was so sad.

I didn't find her that day, but once that summer I saw her sitting beneath the weeping cherry tree. She was small and thin with enormous sorrowful eyes, and she was crying pitifully. I hurried to her but when I reached out to her she wasn't there.

15

It was June 1951. I was eleven, Angel nine. We were sitting on the stoop playing with our Topsy Turvey dolls when a brand-new Buick turned down our street and pulled into the driveway. Polished. Gray. Shiny chrome looked like it might be flashing secret messages to the sun.

Grandmommy hollered, "Hon, come quick, Betty Lou is home." Then she told Angel and me, "Come see your mama." Mama? She was the prettiest lady I'd ever seen. She looked like a movie star. Hair a lot redder than it used to be, like fire shining in the sunlight. Cheeks rouged. Lips orange. She was dressed fit to kill. White suit. Little fur hat cocked off to one side. Had a fur slung round her neck, gray like the alligator purse in her left hand. In her right hand a cigarette in a long silver holder, held in a way that her pinky crooked just right.

Mama stood there in her high-heeled shoes and silk stockings looking like she was *somebody*, so beautiful I was afraid to touch her. Grandmommy pushed me forward until soft, silky fur tickled my cheek. I was rubbing up against the fur, breathing in Mama's sweet-smelling perfume, when I saw little eyes looking at me. I saw little paws. Toenails. Tails. Mama's fur was a little gray squirrel that had been made into a fur scarf, so that the head and two paws ended up over her left breast. All around the back of her neck little tails hung down.

In my mind a fleeting glimpse of another gray squirrel...

The Child:
...For one flickering moment, I remembered Squirrel, jumping from one leafy green tree to another. I remembered his tiny paws taking peanuts from me. I remembered Squirrel. Dead. My heart jumped up into my mouth where it oozed bitter bile. I swallowed and my heart got stuck in my throat. I ran from the dead gray squirrel.

I ran inside, crawled under the bed and hid in the black place inside my head. The memory vanished. I was left only with The Sadness. The Sadness pressed down on me, surrounded me and tried to squeeze the life out of me.

The Other Child:
Grandmommy found me under the bed. "What are you doing under there?"

"I don't know," I said, thinking maybe I was looking for my new shoes to show Mama.

"Come out from under there. Your mama has a surprise."

Some surprise. Mama brought home another man, a thin man who wore glasses. His skin was pale, on account of being indoors all the time, and that made his hair, which was parted right smack in the middle, look even blacker. He wore a white shirt, starched stiff as my extra special petticoat, red suspenders and a bow tie. I couldn't say he looked like anybody I had ever seen before, unless maybe like the pictures I had seen of Teddy Roosevelt or somebody else important.

Mama giggled. "This is Gerald Wilson, your new daddy."

I felt my body stiffen. I stood still as I could, wishing I was invisible. Grandmommy pinched me and whispered, "Don't be so stand-offish." When she pinched me the second time, I understood she wanted me to say something. I said, "Where'd you get *him*?"

"I was playing piano in Alaska, he offered me a job playing in his nightclub, you know, and now we're married. You can call him Daddy if you want."

I went mute. I shook my head and started to walk away.

Mama's new husband said, "When I was a little boy I used to march around in my father's big socks. They called me Socks. You can call me Socks."

Mama said, "Yeah. Sox. With an X"

I was thinking, *At least he doesn't expect me to call him Daddy.*

———————————————◆——————————————

After supper, Mama dusted off the piano and played. I mean she really did play that piano. Her fingers pranced all up and down the keyboard. Mama had a way of throwing back her head when she played and laughing this throaty laugh. We were spellbound.

"Join in," Mama urged. It didn't take much urging on her part, seeing as how Sox had already taken his sax out the case and had been sucking on the reed, getting it ready. Angel ran to get Grandpa's fiddle. Now they all played "When the Saints Go Marching In."

Grandmommy said, "Glory, Hallelujah, Y'all make a joyful noise."

While Mama was playing the piano I noticed her bracelet, and I didn't need anybody to tell me it was real gold. Fact is, it was solid gold. My eyes almost popped out my head to see that mess of gold nuggets all linked together to make a chain for the most magnificent charm bracelet I ever saw or ever will see. Jade dice with gold dots, an ivory Billikan and tiny gold animals dangled from gold links between the nuggets. I knew the Bible said, "Thou shalt not covet," but I wanted that bracelet in the worst way. Mama took off the bracelet and we took turns feeling how heavy it was. You could tell she was glad we were properly impressed.

Grandpa's fiddle sang a tune and the sax answered. They kept up that way, back and forth. We tapped our feet, keeping time. Then Grandpa played "Turkey in the Straw" and pretty soon Angel and I were prancing around the room while Mama, Grandmommy and Sox clapped to the beat. Sox said it was the best "Turkey in the Straw" he ever heard. That was some compliment seeing as how Sox had played with the best, including Lawrence Welk.

For the next day or so, Sox told Grandpa stories of the last frontier, bought Grandmommy groceries, and entertained Angel by placing a cranberry on his lips, pursing his lips like he was whistling, then blowing, so that the cranberry hung in mid-air or danced up and down as he wished. Angel thought he was wonderful and spent hours trying to learn to dance a cranberry on her lips.

Nothing Sox did interested me. I stayed as far away from him as possible.

————————————————

Two days later, Mama and Sox climbed into the new car and drove away. Two hours later, when the Buick pulled back into the driveway, Mama was alone.

Angel gave me a look I couldn't figure. "Mama, where's Sox?" she asked.

"Gone back to Alaska."

"Aren't you going back?"

"Pretty soon."

Angel dropped her head and looked at the ground. "I'm gonna miss you. Sox, too."

"No, you won't 'cause I'm bringing my girls with me."

"Cross your heart?"

"Cross my heart and I hope to die."

Angel jumped up and hightailed it into the house, motioning for me to follow. I followed Angel into the kitchen. Under the sink we found two brown paper bags and on the back porch two more. We stuck the bags up under our skirts and snuck into the bedroom. Angel piled dresses, underwear and socks on the bed. I folded them as neatly as I could and stuffed them into the bags. We snuck out the back door, carted the bags to the car, stowed them on the floor of the back seat and positioned ourselves on the patio between Mama and the new car and waited. We knew that Mama came and went without warning, like a butterfly, landing only long enough to be admired and then flying away.

Now Mama appeared at the front door, and with my own eyes I watched Mama turn into a *witch!* She flew out the front door, down the steps and landed beside us. By then her arms were down at her sides but I knew the truth. What she called Dolman sleeves were not sleeves at all. They were *wings!* I watched her eyes turn from green to gray and in them I saw reflected a tiny me. At first, I thought she meant to shrink us but instead she roared, "What do you think you're doing?"

I didn't say a word. Angel answered, "Putting our bags in the car."

I pinched her. "Blabbermouth."

"Get those bags out of my car," Mama demanded.

"But Mama," Angel said, "it's our clothes. We're packed and ready to go."

"You're not bringing these old things." She passed her hand over our bags, the same way a witch makes a magic spell.

Without thinking, I blurted out, "Mama, are you a witch?"

"Yes," Mama admitted without hesitation. "How do you think I knew you were in my car? I'm a witch, that's how." Mama was whispering so Grandmommy wouldn't hear. She knew Grandmommy didn't allow witches in her house.

Angel's eyes were opened wide. "Is Mama really a witch?" she wanted to know.

"She must be. Mamas don't lie."

That night, before Mama went to bed, she reached into her leather bag and took out a silver flask and a little silver circle. With a flick of her wrist, she turned the piece of silver into a glass from which she drank amber liquid, and then turned the glass back into a round of silver, not much bigger than a dollar. I was thinking, *It must be a magic potion Mama drinks to keep her young.*

After she drank, Mama's face became less strict. She stood at the foot of our bed giggling, then lifted up the covers, stuck her head under the sheet, grabbed my feet and tickled them until I couldn't stand it, then she tickled Angel. Angel laughed so loud Grandpa came to the door. "What's going on in there?"

Mama put her finger to her lips to shush us. She plopped down on the twin bed next to the one I shared with Angel and, just like that, she fell asleep. She slept with her mouth open and from that dark hole came a giant cat-purr sound that frightened Angel but lulled me to sleep.

Next morning, Grandmommy and Grandpa followed us outside. Angel and I stood in the driveway, dressed in our new clothes. Mama sat behind the wheel, impatient to be gone. We had the long drive to Seattle ahead of us. There we would put the new car on a ferry and then catch our flight to Anchorage.

It wasn't until Mama said, "Kiss Grandpa and Grandmommy goodbye," that it dawned on us that we were actually leaving the two people we loved most. Grandmommy dabbed at her eyes. Grandpa shifted his weight from one foot to the other, keeping his eyes focused on some invisible spot just above our heads. A giant tear tore itself loose from inside Angel's belly. It floated up and settled in the hollow place behind her eyes, then burst. Salty teardrops poured out, splattering Grandmommy and making pee-colored splotches on Angel's new yellow dress.

Pickle brine flooded into my chest, squeezing off my heart, forcing itself up into my throat. I pecked Grandpa and Grandmommy on the cheek, grabbed Angel's hand and ran to the car. The pickle brine spilled out and sat on my tongue. It was bitter-sour. I swallowed seven times (a magic number) and trapped it in my throat. Grandpa and Grandmommy stood, waving goodbye as we drove out the driveway. Angel and I knelt on the back seat and watched them until we turned the corner. And then they were gone.

Mama reached over the seat and handed us each a magic wand. When we held our wands near the opened window they twirled and whirled until they became a shiny silver blur. It was perfectly obvious that Mama really was a witch. A good one, I hoped, both frightened and proud. When we finally settled down into the wonderful plushness of the new car, I ran my hands over my stiff new dress, snuck another look at my shiny new shoes and smiled to myself. The way I had it figured, Mama was turning me into something wonderful.

16

Anchorage, Alaska 1951

"The flight to Valdez has been canceled," the man in the blue jacket said. Mama sighed and rolled her eyes. "Canceled? That's impossible."

Blue jacket smiled. "All flights have been canceled because of the wind. I'm afraid you're stuck here, Ma'am."

"You don't know me. One way or another I always get what I want. Right now, I want to get to Valdez." Through clenched teeth, Mama hissed, "C'mon," and marched us onto the airfield, the wind whipping our hair into our faces. Mama asked pilots of small private planes to take us to Valdez. They all said, "No. It's too windy."

Mama wouldn't give up. That's how Mama was. Like a snapping turtle, once she got her teeth into something, she wouldn't let go. Now Mama stuck out her lower lip. "My little girls are exhausted," she said to the next pilot. "Can you take us to Valdez?"

"No. It's too dangerous."

When we got to the last pilot, Mama said, "I'll bet you one hundred dollars you're too chicken-shit to fly to Valdez today." The pilot took the hundred-dollar bill plus four fifties and a ten for the airfare. We climbed into the puny little plane. Behind the seat was a shelf for the luggage. That's where Angel and I sat, squeezed tightly against Mama's suitcases.

We flew over fields of fireweed and lupine, then over willow, spruce and cottonwood. An eagle flew past and perched on the very top of a lone pine. We began to climb. The ground beneath us rose up becoming black, jagged mountains. Now and then the snow-covered peaks mingled with the clouds, and it was hard to tell one from the other. The wind rushed past. The plane lurched, dropped down and tilted to the right, pushing Mama into the window, me into Angel and Angel into the suitcases. The pilot yelled at Mama for talking him into flying, and then no one said anything.

I never knew how big mountains could be or how fragile a plane can be when the wind pushes it here and there. A gust of wind picked up the little plane and carried it towards the mountain on our left. A mountain goat on the ledge stood watching us. The wing caught the tip of a branch and pulled the leaves off. The startled goat turned and scampered away.

The pilot was watching the mountains, his forehead wet with sweat. Mama was watching him sweat, her mouth crooked, her hands busy smoothing down her coat. The pilot said, "Damn wind. 'Cuse. Sonofabitchin' wind. 'Cuse."

The wind howled and whistled, shaking, and bouncing the little plane. At first it was fun getting bounced around, lifted up, then dropped down as if we were up on a mountain of wind and then sliding down. Angel giggled. "This is like a roller coaster." Then a suitcase toppled over, struck her on the forehead and made her cry.

"Tie every sonofabitchin' thing down." Mama reached over the seat and did like the pilot said.

We passed the mountain, then another and another. The wind pushed down on us, pushed us into a nosedive, then up. The plane wobbled. The pilot said, "This is it."

Angel said, "What?"

I said, "He's scared of gettin' thrown against the rocks by the wind."

Mama gave me a dirty look. "We're not getting thrown anywhere. We've got the best damn pilot there ever was."

The pilot said, "Damn right."

We passed the mountains and dropped down. Mama pointed. "Valdez."

"I see her."

"There's the strip." Mama pointed. Valdez was surrounded by mountains on three sides and by the ocean on the west. The landing strip ran right down to the Pacific. We went bump bump on the strip. The wind wouldn't let us land. It got under the plane and lifted us up. We had to fly up again or we would have gone smack dab into the ocean. We circled round and tried again. And again. The pilot said, "Sonofabitch. Sonofabitch, we're gonna run outta fuel."

Mama's chin was puckered up, her mouth flopped over to one side and her top teeth were pressed into her lower lip. "We could land at Robe Lake."

"Chrissake, why the hell didn't you tell me before?"

Mama told the pilot how to get to Robe Lake and the pilot set the little amphibian down on the water, and somebody, I don't remember who, gave us a ride into Valdez.

It was late afternoon when the car stopped in front of Club Valdez. "We're home," Mama said.

"Well, look what the wind blew in," said the man behind the bar. "I can't believe you flew with the girls in this wind." He turned to me and Angel. "Welcome to Valdez," he said. It was Sox. Mama twirled around so he could admire her, then made a half curtsy, in acknowledgment of the admiration she expected. Next, she pointed to the pilot like it was his turn to take a bow. "Give this man a drink on the house." Then Mama told the story of how he came to be the best damn pilot there ever was. The weary pilot went straight to the bar and began a three-day drunk and the saga of the sonofabitching wind.

Mama perched on a barstool. Angel and I climbed up on stools of our own.

Angel said, "Coke. On the rocks."

I said, "Seven up. With a twist."

Sox said we shouldn't be at the bar and that got him started off on the wrong foot with Mama. To make matters worse, Mama's glass wasn't filled to suit her. She hopped off the barstool, went round behind the bar, topped off the drink, stomped back to her stool and drank it down in one gulp. Sox reached for the glass to refill it. Mama was feeling ornery and wouldn't let go of the glass. Sox shrugged. "Suit yourself," he said as he walked away. Mama climbed off the stool, went round behind the bar and poured herself another drink.

Once the drinks hit bottom, Mama forgot she was peeved and paraded me and Angel around the bar, making a spectacle of us, then arranged us at the centermost table where we'd be in plain view. Sox brought another round of drinks and ordered dinner, the likes of which we'd never seen before. Alaska king crab. Steamed clams. Filet mignon. And Cook made Baked Alaska for dessert. "Welcome to Alaska," he said, bringing us fancy ice cream.

After dinner Mama took us to the house across the street, and sent us to bed.

"But it's still daytime," Angel said.

"We're in the land of the midnight sun," Mama said, "It doesn't get dark. Get to bed." She headed back to the club.

The house was built up on stilts and sat on the tide flat so that when the tide was in, the water was all around us and underneath the house. At first we were scared, alone in a strange place with the ocean underneath us, lapping at the posts, but after while the gentle sound lulled us to sleep.

◆━━━━◆━━━━◆

Next morning, Angel pulled back the drapes and we discovered a magical place. On the other side of the window a boardwalk connected us to the tide flat. The boards had been weathered and bleached by the salt air like driftwood. We knelt on our beds and peered out. The sun shone down, reflecting on the receding tide. The wet sand shimmered, as if it were sprinkled with ten thousand diamonds. A seagull swooped down and snatched a silvery fish, then perched on one of the pilings not more than five feet away, while his kinfolk soared overhead, plummeting headlong, nearly to their death, then rose again to ride the wind.

We stayed that way, gazing out the window, until our stomachs complained of neglect. We found a note on the kitchen table, next to the cereal box, telling us to eat breakfast, and warning us to be quiet until Mama and Sox woke up.

"Angel, make up your bed, " I said. "I don't think Mama will do it for us like Grandmommy used to do." When I said that, I tasted salt. I caught the tears in my throat and swallowed them. I missed Grandmommy and Grandpa something terrible.

Mama woke at noon, reaching for the cigarettes on her bedside table. Her ashtray, a free-form chrome blob, was overflowing with dead cigarettes. By the time coffee was made, she had two or three live ones burning, all at the same time, and scattered all over the house.

Angel and I greeted Mama with an exuberant "Good morning."

Mama grumbled, "Don't talk to me until I've had my coffee."

Mama had dark pouches underneath her eyes. Her mouth drooped. She plopped down and sat, hunched over the kitchen table. She lit another cigarette. Poured a cup of coffee. I noticed she no longer used sugar and cream. She drank her coffee black, sometimes laced with whiskey.

She stayed like that, bent over, drinking coffee and smoking cigarettes, until time for work. She was hung over, cranky and in no mood to talk. Angel and I learned to stay out of Mama's way until Mama sought us out, which was after she was dressed and on the way out the door. "See you at supper," she would say.

Mama planned to cook us supper every night, and she did, too, until the novelty wore off. That took three days. After that, we ate at the Club.

Mama and Sox fought like alley cats. It was plumb crazy the way they carried on, cussing, calling each other names you wouldn't call a rabid dog. They disagreed about everything, even the one thing that could have brought them closer together- their music. Like now. Mama said, "The crowd sure went wild over my piano last night."

"You must be blind," Sox said. "Couldn't you tell they were crazy for the sax?"

Mama got up, slammed the door, stomped across the street, yanked the Club's heavy drapes off the windows and sent them to the cleaners, then took down the Venetian blinds and lugged them home to soak. Bending over the bathtub, which was filled with hot water and ammonia, she scrubbed the heavy blinds, breathing in ammonia fumes.

"You shouldn't be doing that," Sox said. "You're pregnant." Under his breath he said, "And ornerier than ever." He walked out the door.

Pregnant? Mama didn't look pregnant to me.

Now Mama was standing in the doorway, not moving, her face white. She clutched her crotch. Her hand came away red. Blood!...

The Child:
...I remembered that other blood. The blood goes drip, drip, drip on the floor. The blood makes a pool on the floor and the blood pool is getting bigger. There was a scream inside my throat but it couldn't get out. I shut my eyes real tight. I couldn't see the blood any more. There was nothing but quiet black space...

...I was standing in front of Mama. She was standing in the doorway in a puddle of blood, her face white. I had no idea how I came to be there.

It had happened before, the strange sensation of having just popped into being. It was like I didn't even exist, and then there I was.

I stepped over the blood and ran to get help. I was thinking, *If a bad man hurt Mama, I might have to kill him.*

Mama named the baby Zoe. "Just look at how *petite* she is," Mama gushed. Zoe had a darling little round face but she was awfully small. Mama thought Zoe was perfect, not tall and skinny like me, not chubby like Angel. It was easy to see that we'd never measure up.

Valdez, Alaska 1953

Two years had gone by. I was thirteen. I got my period. I grew breasts. I swiped Mama's black lace bra off the clothesline, slipped on a sweater and, sticking out in front, strutted into the kitchen, proud as all get out. Mama looked at me with cold ice-green eyes, her face frozen, her lips pinched tightly together, and I knew Mama was not happy about me filling out her bra.

Mama sat bent over the kitchen table wearing her morning-after face, puffing on a cigarette. Zoe sat in Mama's lap playing with Mama's silver cigarette lighter. Zoe was two years old now with big green eyes and bouncy red curls tumbling onto her little round face. Cute little thing, they said, too bad Betty's got her spoiled rotten.

Mama especially liked Zoe because she had red hair. Mama's came out of a bottle, and once I saw her washing Zoe's hair with the same stuff. "That proves I'm a *natural* redhead," Mama would say. "How else would Zoe get red hair?"

Angel was blonde so Mama left her alone. She was after me constantly. "Don't you want auburn hair?" she asked again and again.

I wondered, *Would Mama love me more if I had red hair?*

———————————————

Mama poured herself a cup of coffee, took a sip and set it aside.

I was sitting at the kitchen table working on a jigsaw puzzle. The tide was in and I could hear the water splashing against the pilings. Mama reached for the VO. "You're old enough to drink," she told me. "I'm gonna teach you to do it right." Mama went to the cupboard, took down a bottle of scotch and poured two water glasses full. "Just add water, or ice. One cube. Never anything sweet." She handed me a glass. She drank hers straight.

I thought about what Grandmommy would think. And Jesus. But I took a sip anyway, just to please Mama. I hated the taste. And Mama could tell. She looked at me in that disapproving way, like I had never done anything right my whole life.

———————————————

Mister Stout, my 7th grade teacher, stopped by the house. "Lucinda should skip eighth grade and go straight to high school," he said.

Mama tightened her mouth. "Absolutely not."

Sox sighed like somebody tired of having to argue over every little thing. "Why not let her?"

"Because, you know, just because."

Sox said, "She'll get in college sooner."

Mama lit a cigarette. "She's not *that* smart." Mama chewed on her lower lip, took a drag and blew the smoke in my direction.

"She's quite the student," Mister Stout said.

Me? The Student?

Outnumbered, Mama mumbled, "Well, she can't just skip a grade."

Sox said, "I'll hire a tutor."

The Student:
...Sox hired a tutor who introduced me to Frost, Sandburg and T. S. Elliot. Wanting not to be like the hollow men, headpiece stuffed with straw, I finished eighth grade in three weeks. In less time than that, Mama had made arrangements to get rid of me.

"You'll be better off attending high school *Outside*,"[7] she said.

"If you're mad about the bra," I said, "I'll give it back."

"Don't be ridiculous. I don't want it." Mama stomped off in a huff. "You can have the raggedy old thing."

I was thinking, *Maybe I would be better off with auburn hair.*

---

7. Alaskans refer to any non-Alaskan location, including other U.S. states as "Outside."

18

Grants Pass, Oregon 1953

I didn't mind the long walk to school. September brought cool, crisp mornings and glorious afternoons. The leaves, vivid orange and scarlet, clashed against a bright blue sky. I breathed deeply. There was a rich heavy smell in the air, the full-bodied fragrance of ripe grapes, earth recently turned and ready for the planting of bulbs and the smell of fresh bread baking. I heard the honking of geese overhead and raised my eyes upwards. I could not see the geese but I knew they were headed south.

I walked quickly past the hospital and the funeral hall and down the hill, sprinting the last few blocks so I could hang out at the school store before school, listening to the jukebox crank out Theresa Brewer. I stood in the corner watching the pretty girls giggling and whispering. I wanted to be one of *them. They* wore pleated skirts and sweater sets. They had ponytails, pageboys, or short hair with Mamie Eisenhower bangs. I wore homemade cotton print skirts and blouses, and my long, dark hair hung loosely around my shoulders.

The Sadness snuck up behind me and hissed, "You stick out like a boil on a snake's ass."

I did look different, but I had the feeling it was more than that, more than the hair or the clothes, more than the whispered, "She comes from a broken family."

Something was out of kilter.

The bell rang. I walked across the street to the school. Each time the buzzer sounded, three hundred pairs of feet thundered to the next class. I had six teachers, one for each subject. They bored me with their tedious monologues, and I surely didn't impress them, as I sat gazing out the window.

On Friday, the bell rang at an odd time. We left our seats and swarmed across the street towards a large brick building with "Gymnasium" stamped above the door.

I could hear a drum pounding out a marching beat.

"Where we going?" I asked no one in particular.

Scarlet lips smiled down at me and said, "Pep Rally."

"What's that?" I asked the lips dominating the small, round face six inches north of mine. The face was pale and fringed with black hair. Strangely, the too-bright lips were just the right touch.

"Stick with me, Kid. You've been in Alaska too long."

"How'd you know?" I asked.

And Lorelei, that was her name, said, "Everybody knows. It's a small school."

"Small? This school is almost as large as the *town* I lived in."

"They say you're the youngest kid in the whole school. How old are you anyway?"

"Thirteen."

"You don't look thirteen."

I hoped she thought I looked older. Lorelei most certainly did. Not only was she tall, she filled out her black sweater and skirt very nicely. She was eighteen, a Senior, and hung with older boys, already out of school. A wild crowd.

We were inside now. The drum was very loud. Eight pretty girls appeared from nowhere. Identical, like they were cut from one piece of paper. I stared at the one closest to me. Hair the color of wheat touched by moonlight. Blue eyes. Pink pouting lips. She wore a short blue skirt and a white sweater with a thick blue G emphasizing her breasts. Blue laces crisscrossed white suede shoes Lorelei called "white bucks." The dancing dolls led the Pep Rally, waving, shaking pom poms. Whirling. Twirling. Getting everybody all worked up.

Adults, especially teachers, always ask you what you want to be when you grow up. Now I knew. I wanted to be a cheerleader.

Lorelei took me to cheerleading try outs, lent me money for my outfit, talked Grandmommy into letting me go to the football games and convinced her to let me go to the Sock Hop. In my socks, on the smooth slippery gym floor, I felt like I was just like everybody else. I learned to Bunny Hop in a long boy-girl, boy-girl line. Right foot kicking, left foot kicking, a jump and a jump and a hop, hop, hop. A boy took my hand and led me to a large circle. I put my right hand in, I put my right hand out, I put my right hand in and shook it all about, then I put my hip in and shook it. It was naughty, and I knew it, but I did the Hokey Pokey anyway.

Then suddenly the music was muffled and sounded far away. I seemed to glide away from the others until I stood apart watching them, faces blurred, moving in slow motion, sounding like buzzing insects. I closed my eyes. I felt like I was floating up up up near the ceiling...

...I opened my eyes, surprised to find myself in a boy girl boy girl circle. Sometimes it happened like that, and I felt like I just wasn't there half the time, like I drifted in and out of existence, here one minute, gone the next.

"Do the Hokey Pokey," the music said. I sat down.

"Why aren't you dancing?" somebody said. "They're doing the Hokey Pokey."

But I didn't know how.

———————◆———◆———◆———————

I was running across the field to cheerleading practice when I overheard a boy tell his friend that I was *sexy*. I was fourteen and I wasn't sure what that meant until the following Sunday when I came across a photograph of Marilyn Monroe in the newspaper. "Sexy Marilyn Monroe running to meet Joe DiMaggio," the paper said. *So that's what sexy is*, I thought, taking in the flirty smile, the voluptuous body and the tight dress. Now I wanted to *be* Marilyn Monroe. I cut Marilyn Monroe out of the paper and studied her. Eyebrows plucked and arched. Beauty spot. Dark red lips. Hair falling down over one eye.

Oddly, that night before bed, when I looked in the mirror, I saw that my eyebrows were plucked, the mole near my left eye had been darkened with an eyebrow pencil, my long dark hair was brushed across one eye and my lips were painted dark red. "Angel," I said, "Look at my eyebrows."

"You plucked 'em."

"I did? Did you see me?" I tried to remember. Had I done it and forgotten? I stood staring at the strange new me in the mirror, both excited and frightened at the change in myself. "You're weird," Angel said, "And you better get that lipstick off before Grandpa sees it."

I scrubbed my lips clean so Grandpa wouldn't see the new me and waited until I got to school to put on my new face. I knew now that I could be anybody I wanted to be, changing what I wore, how I wore it, like I was a paper doll or something.

The next day, after gym, I pulled my hair back into a ponytail and stepped into the shower. The other girls stared at me. "What are you staring at?"

One girl said, "You look different."

Another said, "You're built like a brick shithouse and not a brick out of place."

Tears stinging my eyes, I stumbled out of the shower, embarrassed and ashamed.

"What's wrong?" Lorelei asked.

"That girl said I look like a toilet." I wiped at my tears.

Lorelei went to talk to the girl, then came back and explained, "She means you have a nice figure. Don't you know you look good?"

"I'm ugly."

"Kid, you got no self-confidence," Lorelei told me, "Come with me." Lorelei grabbed my arm, dragged me into the locker room and stood me in front of the mirror. "Take off your clothes. I bet you've never looked at yourself naked before."

I shook my head.

"Well, it's time you did."

I stared at the body in the mirror. My breast were round, my waist small, my hips nicely rounded and firm. Lorelei sucked in her breath and let it out in a whistle. "Damn girl, no wonder they call you 'the body'."

The one in the mirror they called "The Body" winked at me. I felt my face turn red hot. I watched the face in the mirror change color.

———————◆———————◆———————

Lorelei sauntered across the street to the school store, swinging her hips side to side. She had spotted some college boys she knew and wanted to be sure they saw her. I followed, walking with my head down. I didn't want to be noticed.

Lorelei sidled up to the yellow convertible.

I went into the store and ordered a cherry coke. I was rummaging around in my purse for a dime when out the corner of my eye I saw the man in a checkered jacket. The coke flew from my hand and crashed to the ground. Glass splintered. Coke splattered. I ran out without paying.

Now my legs turned wobbly. "Mama!" I heard a little girl scream just before I fell headlong into the street.

Lorelei hovered over my still body. "What's the matter? Can you breathe? Take a breath."

"That man. He was looking at me."

"What do you care? Do you know him? What's his name?"

I searched the corners of my mind. *Who is the man in the checkered jacket?*

Lorelei propped me up on the bench just outside the store. I sat, slumped over, trying hard to remember the man in the checked jacket. I remembered nothing.

Now Lorelei walked quickly towards the convertible, mumbling something to the college boys. I couldn't make it out. The college boys came running.

Lorelei grabbed my arm and tried to pull me to my feet. "C'mon, show us where he is. "

"Noooo. I'm not gonna. Lemme go."

The college boys, one on each side, put arms under my armpits and drug me back inside the store. "Where is he?"

I pointed. The man in the checkered jacket turned. I shut my eyes.

"Open your eyes," Lorelei demanded. "Open your eyes."

I opened my eyes. I saw big lumberjack boots. Levis. Checkered jacket. Black and red. Blood red. It would be scratchy, I knew. *Hands rough. Stinky rotten whiskey breath.*

"Look at his face," Lorelei said. "Who is it?"

Slowly I raised my eyes. *Whiskers like pricker branches.* Grinning mouth. Nostrils flared. My heart chugged along like a freight train. *I'm scared to see them yellow eyes.* Louder now and speeding up, my heart went chug. Chug. Chug.

"He's a bad man." The voice coming out of my mouth was the voice of a child. "He's got a gun," the child whispered, "He's got a sharp knife. His name is Clay Stout."

Darkness pummeled me without warning.

I opened my eyes. I was lying on Lorelei's bed unable to remember how I got there. I was shaking and couldn't stop. "Look at her," I heard one of the college boys say, "She's scared to death. I wish it would've been that sonofabitch. I'd like to pound my fist in his face. I'd like to kill him."

"Oh, yes. Let's kill him," I said, grabbing the boy's hand. "Let's find him and kill him." I looked into the boy's eyes. They were not the cold eyes of a killer.

I'd have to do it myself.

19

June 1954

Mama came and went like a tornado. She'd whirl into town with no warning, twirl around, disrupt everything around her and then disappear. This time would be no different. When I got home from school there was a shiny black Buick parked in the driveway. Mama sat, leaning against the horsehair sofa, smoking a cigarette, her feet resting on a footstool.

Mama had Zoe with her. Zoe was two and a half years old now, her curls the same fiery red as Mama's. They were wearing yellow sundresses with white diagonal stripes. Zoe wore sunglasses, like Mama, and carried a tiny white patent leather purse.

"There you are," Mama said. Like always, she made no move to hug me. I reached out to Zoe. Zoe stuck her finger in her mouth and hid behind Mama's skirt. "Leave her alone," Mama said.

"Nice to have a baby sister that doesn't even know you," Angel said. Angel's eyes took in the new car, the fancy clothes and Mama's matched set of luggage. "Must be nice to be rich."

Mama grinned.

"How come you never buy nice clothes for me and Lucinda?"

"Oh, I did," Mama said. "I bought you some outfits to wear on the trip."

"What trip?"

"It's a surprise."

We knew better than to press Mama for details. She'd say anything that came into her mind *if* she wanted to but if she didn't, you couldn't pry it from her. She could be as closed mouth as a bear trap that had sprung and was locked tight. We would have to wait until Mama was good and ready to tell.

"Mama, do you want some more coffee?" Angel said, smoothing down her skirt.

Mama didn't answer.

At six o'clock the next morning, Mama burst into the room, her lips pressed tightly together. "Get up. Get dressed. Let's get going."

"Gosh darn it," Angel said. "I didn't get to say goodbye to my friends." she had tears in her eyes.

Mama grabbed my arm, digging in her nails. "Did you hear me? Get dressed. Now!"

I jerked away. "But I want to—" It was no use. I knew Mama didn't care what I wanted.

"I miss Grandmommy and Grandpa already," Angel said.

———————— •┼━━━┼• ————————

When we got to Valdez, Mama headed straight to the bar and perched on a barstool, resting her left heel on the highest rung of the stool, her right leg crossed over the left, so that her legs were drawn up, and in that position her short, tight skirt barely covered her reason why. That's what Grandmommy called what you got between your legs. I once asked Grandmommy why she called it that, and she said, "It's our reason why we mustn't go naked."

Mama poured herself a drink. I reached over, tugged at her skirt, and whispered, "Mama, your skirt is too short." I was thinking, *I wish Mama would act like a mama should.*

Mama's face hardened. Her eyes narrowed and became acid green slits. She drew back her hand and slapped me across the face. I felt my face redden. I stood perfectly still, looking at my blurry mama through watery eyes. Embarrassed, I closed my eyes and pretended I wasn't there...

———————————————•—◆—•———————————————

The Protector:

..."What did I do wrong?" I said. "You're the one with your reason why on display." I made my right hand into a fist and took a step towards Mama.

Sox scooted out from behind the bar and stood between us. "C'mon. I'll take you home," he said, "Angel's tired." I left without saying a word. I didn't talk after we got home either. I went straight to bed and lay staring at the ceiling, listening to the gentle sound of the waves lapping against the pilings, thinking about how I came to be back in Alaska and how every time I got settled Mama uprooted me again. I had nothing to say about it. Nobody ever asked me how I felt, or what I wanted. I felt numb, like a dead thing. Then a strange thing happened. I felt like I had left my body and floated up and hovered up against the ceiling. It was quite pleasant to float, weightless, feeling nothing. After a while I floated down, down, down- light as a feather, into my body where I fell immediately into a deep sleep...

———————————————•—◆—•———————————————

Uncle Edward was living in Valdez now. Mama claimed he followed her up to Alaska. Uncle Edward swore he was there first, had come up with the Marines. Him being the more reliable, I'd go with his version.

Uncle Edward's beautiful young wife painted her fingernails scandalous red to match her full pouty mouth. Blonde, her hair grazed her waist. Natural, brown-eyed blondes are as hard to find as a toad without warts but you could tell Uncle Edward's wife was blonde all over. She was *very* nice. That summer Uncle Edward found out just how nice she was to the longshoremen. He put her on a plane, told her, "Don't come back," and filed for a divorce.

Uncle Edward moped for a month or so and then went "outside" to cry on Grandmommy's shoulder. Grandmommy introduced him to the preacher's daughter. Patsy was even more beautiful than the blonde. She had thick dark hair that fell past her shapely hips. She wore no make-up. She didn't need any. Patsy was nice but not in a way so as to cause concern, so Uncle Edward married her.

I had known Patsy from high school, and we had gone to the same church in Grants Pass. We were good friends.

It was November and barely light as we walked to school, and already darkening when we left at three. I hurried home.

"Mama, can I go to the picture show?" I asked.

"You're grown. You don't have to ask me if you can go out and you don't have to be in at any certain time, just tell me where you're going."

"Grown?" Sox shook his head. "She's *fourteen*. No curfew? Good way to get her to be a slut like her mother."

I was glad Mama thought I was grown up, but I wasn't sure how I'd know when to come home. I figured I could ask the other girls when they had to be home and pretend my curfew was the same. I didn't want people talking about me like they did Mama. "Betty's sneaking around with Bill, the longshore foreman," they said. "They're so steamed up over each other they just might melt the Glacier, wonder why Gerry doesn't throw her out."

Mama didn't care what they said. If Mama saw something she wanted, she went after it, even if it belonged to somebody else.

I was glad for an excuse to get out of the house.

After the movie, I walked home slowly, along the snow-covered path, feeling strangely at peace in the black winter night. Northern Lights appeared above me. I had seen them before, of course, sometimes a pale swatch of luminous white or a patch of bluish green, sometimes a flash across the sky. This time, unearthly Aurora Borealis appeared from nowhere, ghostly lights, glowing against the navy-blue sky, illuminating the night, dancing translucent blue-green ribbons, shining with supernatural light.

Each step I took made a loud crunching sound that clashed against the still and peaceful night. It began to snow. The flakes fell gently.

20

Molalla, Oregon 1955

When I was fifteen, Mama and Sox sold Club Valdez and we moved into a big white farmhouse with a porch, barn filled with hay and kittens, a few dozen sheep grazing in the pasture and crayfish in the creek.

"We're gonna be happy here," Mama promised.

"I'm going for a walk," I said.

Hardly any people were out, on account of how hot it was. I walked alone, carrying the Sadness piggyback down the deserted street. I was walking fast, looking straight ahead but not seeing, when a collie ran across the street in front of me. A fragmented memory ambushed me...

The Child:

...I'm walking down a path looking for Lyptus. The wind blows and the leaves rustle in the trees. I look up expecting to see Squirrel. I hear

someone cry. I stop and listen. I can hear the cries of a little girl. They seem a long way off. I tip-toe on down the path. I see a shadowy lump ahead, then I see the dog with the neat little bullet hole in its head. Blood. So much blood.

I retreated into the black space inside my head and fell, spinning and twirling, end over end, into a black bottomless pit inside myself...

The following year, Grandpa sold his house and built a small house next door. The next to come was Uncle Edward and Patsy, then Uncle Matt, Charlotte and my two little girl cousins. They set up trailer houses over under the maple trees.

Grandmommy insisted we all join the Evangelical Church over by the river, which was handy for baptizing, and put us to work for the Lord. Uncle Matt was choir director, Uncle Edward, Patsy and I sang in the choir, and Mama played organ.

Uncle Matt was planning an Easter sunrise service with five, maybe six, churches taking part. He asked Mama to play the big organ at the Methodist church where we rehearsed. That's where I met J.D.

J.D. showed up in the middle of our third rehearsal, and, without a word, joined the choir. During break he announced, "I'm singing a solo."

Uncle Matt was amused. You could tell by the way the corners of his mouth turned up. "And what will you sing?"

J.D. burst into song, singing something from "The Messiah" and even the most accomplished singers knew they would be taking a back seat.

You would've known J.D. was from California the moment you laid eyes on him in his tight Levis, his black leather jacket (that he wore everywhere he went) his collar turned up, no socks and his hair slicked back in a "duck's ass." It was the necktie you couldn't figure. It didn't make any sense at all until he took it off right after rehearsal, then you knew the necktie was his way of dressing up, wanting to make a good impression when he met Uncle Matt.

After rehearsal, J.D. sidled up next to me and stared boldly. "Bitchin' sweater," he said.

Sox called J.D. a punk, said he walked with a California swagger. It might have been because one leg was shorter than the other, on account of his mother was snowed in when she was pregnant and didn't have anything to eat except potatoes.

Every time Grandmommy saw J.D. she mumbled, "Lord, have mercy."

Mama said, "I think he's cute."

By Easter J.D. and I were going steady.

On Easter morning Mama whacked several inches of fabric off the bottom of her sea green suit and made herself a hat, then she wadded up some green netting and tacked it onto the hat so that some draped across her forehead. It was the darndest thing I'd ever seen called a hat, yet on Mama it looked good. She stepped into green alligator shoes and stood in front of the mirror, arranging three large green orchids, interspersed with a spray of smaller white orchids, so they climbed up her left breast. "Mama," she called to Grandmommy, "Come see my corsage."

Grandmommy studied the flowers. "What are they?"

"The large are "Emerald Isle" cattaleya orchids, and the smaller ones are Odontoglossum Crispin orchids- the same ones Princess Margaret wore. See?" Mama showed Grandmommy a picture in a magazine.

"I thought Sox bought you a corsage. Where is it?"

Mama rolled her eyes and jerked her head towards the refrigerator.

I slipped into white linen with tiny gold buttons marching down the front and stepped into my first high heels. I couldn't wait to show Mama. I thought maybe she'd be proud that I looked grown up. Mama looked at me with stingy eyes. "Your dress is too tight. Go change. And take off those heels."

I turned and headed back to my room to change. Grandmommy took my arm and turned me around. "Betty Lou, look how nice your daughter looks. Don't you just love her dress?"

Mama didn't answer.

"Grandmommy, do you think it's too tight?" I asked.

Grandmommy stared past me, looking Mama right in the eye. "I do not."

Then Sox came into the room with corsages for us me and Angel, and Grandmommy pinned on the white orchid Sox had picked for me. "Perfect," she said.

Mama pooched out her lower lip and hardened her eyes, looking at me in some kind of new way that I didn't like.

21

Less than a month after we started dating, J.D and I had a fight, and he took off and hitchhiked to San Francisco. Two weeks later he called. "Come to Frisco," he begged. "Come down and marry me. It's bitchin' down here."

"I don't want to get married," I said.

"Let me talk to Betty."

Mama talked private with J.D. for about ten minutes, then hung up and announced that I was getting married. She had finally figured out a way to get rid of me for good.

Grandpa grumbled, "J.D.'s nothin' but a dad-burned whipper-snapper."

Grandmommy dabbed at her eyes with a handkerchief. "Sweet Jesus, Betty Lou, how can J.D. support a wife?"

Mama got the hard look and stuck out her chin.

"J.D. doesn't even have a pot to piss in. How can you even think about letting her marry him?" Sox doubled up his fist and raised his hand to Mama. Came close to hitting her, too, but walked away, swearing under his breath.

All of which is to say that no one thought I should get married, except Mama, who took me aside and told me she thought it was best, then she bought a one-way ticket to San Francisco and put me on the bus.

The Sadness sat next to me on the bus, crept inside me, squeezing tears from my heart. The tears overflowed, poured out my eyes and ran down my cheeks. I rested my forehead on the window, sniffling. Tears mixed with snot. I wiped my nose with the back of my hand, then wiped it on the seat. The woman sitting next to me got up and moved to the back of the bus. In the window glass I could see that I looked pitiful. Eyes puffy. Nose red. My head down 'cause Mama was sending me off to get married before I was grown.

J.D. was nothing to brag about. On probation for armed robbery, he claimed he was framed, but he had a small scar on his back and a large one in his belly where the bullet tore through his body when a cop shot him as he fled the scene of a felony.

On the other hand, J.D. had told me he wanted to be a minister. I was thinking, *Being a minister's wife wouldn't be so bad. I could keep the parsonage clean, and I would like it if people came to me and told me their troubles.*

Little did I know my own troubles were just beginning.

Things did not go well in San Francisco. That's a whole other story I won't tell at this time. The long and short of it is that I wanted to go home. I climbed up into the bus, relieved that it was over but, at the last minute, J.D. climbed on the bus and sat down next to me.

Mama met us at the bus station.

"I'm not getting married," I stated emphatically.

Mama pressed her lips tightly together. She turned to J.D. "Where shall I drop you?"

"I'll just come to your house," he said.

You might think Mama would have taken me aside and asked what happened and whether or not I wanted J.D. to stay. Instead, she ignored me like always. "You can sleep on the cot in the basement tonight," she told J.D.

That night, when I heard Sox snoring and I figured everybody was asleep, I headed for the basement to tell J.D. I didn't want to see him anymore. I crept down the stairs in the dark and tiptoed across the living room into the kitchen. As I started down the basement stairs, I bumped into Mama sneaking up the stairs, her hair rumpled, her face flushed.

"What are you doing here?" Mama asked, surprised to see me.

"What are *you* doing?" I asked. I didn't really want to know what Mama had been doing down in the basement in the dark, in her nightgown, with J.D. I hid what I knew in that black secret place inside my head so I wouldn't have to deal with Mama's betrayal.

I remembered only that I started down to the basement and changed my mind.

M ama had never mentioned our dad. Now that Angel was asking to see him, Mama couldn't find one good thing to say about him. "Why would you want to find Merle? He's nothing but a sloppy ole Swede."

Angel stomped her foot. "I want my dad. Why won't you tell me how I can find him?"

"We don't need Merle," I said, "We've got Sox."

"It's not the same. I want my own dad."

For two months Angel pestered Mama, day and night. Finally, Mama agreed to write Merle and see if he would come.

Angel whispered in my ear, "How does Mama know how to get hold of him? She told us he left us, and she didn't know where he was."

I shrugged my shoulders. "He probably won't come anyway. I'm not holding my breath."

Angel got herself all dressed up in her favorite purple dress. Brushed her hair until it was all fluffy and soft, looking like a golden cloud sitting on her head. I tied a purple ribbon in her hair.

She stared at herself in the mirror. "Do I look all right?"

"You look fine," I said. And she did.

I changed into my pink dress. It was too tight. The red dress was, too. I settled on the blue.

I looked out the window. Nothing. "He's not coming," I said. Angel's bottom lip quivered. "Well, maybe he will," I said quickly.

Mama had always referred to Merle as "that sloppy ole Swede" so it was a jolt when we finally met him. He stood tall as when he was in the Marines and dressed as neatly as he had in the Navy. Thirty-three years old, he had a boyish look about him. A shock of blonde hair. The same hazel eyes as Angel. Angel trailed along behind him, grinning. Thunderstruck. "Dad, come see my room. Dad, do you want cream in your coffee?" Dad this. Dad that.

"Isn't he great?" she whispered.

I didn't answer. I sat on the edges of my chair, fidgeting, not knowing what to say. And when I called him "Dad", it stuck to my tongue and sounded strange to my ears. I called him "Merle".

Merle took a sip of his coffee. "You girls have grown up to be fine young ladies." I felt my face redden. I was thinking, *I'm not so nice. I'm three months along.* It wasn't the first thing I wanted my long lost dad to know. I was pregnant and unmarried. I had broken up with J.D. and even now, with a baby on the way, I didn't want to marry him.

———————◆———————

God bless the Salvation Army Home for Unwed Mothers.

I sat on the wide wooden porch with other young girls with swollen bellies, staring off into space. Sometimes a tear escaped and rolled down a puffy cheek. I pretended I didn't see their tears and when it was my turn to cry, the other girls pretended they didn't see mine.

I shared my cheerful yellow room with an older girl. She shook her head slowly from side to side. "I don't understand how you kids got here."

A girl the color of licorice explained, "The same way you did, honey, we was fuckin'. You know what do it."

Major Brakenstein, a large square woman, solid as a German tank, with legs like telephone poles, ran the home like a military base. Behind her back we called her Major Frankenstein.

Major Frankenstein saw to it that we got up at six o'clock every morning, made our beds, showered and dressed. After breakfast, she herded us down a long white corridor to the clinic. Beyond the clinic, behind closed doors, was the hospital. One by one, girls were taken there. We could hear them scream. A baby cry. We never saw them again.

The Social Worker clicked her tongue against the roof of her mouth. "Tsk, tsk, children having children." She looked at me and shook her head. "You can't keep your baby. You're only sixteen. You are too young to take care of a baby."

"I can take care of a baby. I'm keeping it."

She looked at me with sad eyes. "How did it happen? How did a nice girl like you get in a family way?"

"Well, J.D. likes to quote stuff out of the Bible. He said he was going to be a minister. I didn't think a God-fearing Baptist would try to go all the way, then one time we were necking and he started to do more. I was so surprised I didn't know what to do. Afterwards, I was afraid that if we broke up, he might tell the other boys and I'd get a bad reputation."

"What about *your* feelings?"

I shrugged. "Men do what they want. You can't stop them."

It was November, the ground cold and hard, the trees naked, the leaves covered with frost. Merle's ship was in. He brought me a box of chocolates and sat with me on the Salvation Army porch drinking Coca Cola and looking out across the lawn. Knowing I liked to watch the birds, he had scattered sunflower seeds on the ground and the birds came. "Woodpecker," he said, pointing to a small black and white bird with a long beak and a patch of red on top its head. I smiled. Merle smiled back.

"I'm sorry I wasn't around when you were little," he said. "I did try to see you. Betty wouldn't let me."

I reached into the black place inside my head and pulled out a long forgotten memory. *I'm in a bus with Mama. A sailor comes running up to the bus hollering "I want to see my daughter, dammit, let me see my little girl. "Mama tells the bus driver, "He's drunk, let's go". The sailor tries to get on the bus but the bus driver shuts the door so he can't get in. The sailor pounds on the door. The bus driver calls the police. My face glued against the glass, I watch the police drag him away. He's yelling my name. "Mama," I say, "who's that?"* The memory flashed quickly through my mind. "I remember," I told the dad I never knew.

"Did you get the watch I dropped off at your grandparents for your birthday? I caught the dickens from your mother for that."

"A watch?" My mind wandered back to 1950. *I'm ten. It's dark out. I hear a thump on the porch. I open the door. A taxicab drives slowly by. A drunken sailor hangs out the window, calling my name. There's a package on the stoop. Scrawled on the package in large block letters is: Lucinda, Happy Birthday from your darling Dad.*

Grandmommy grabs the package out of my hands. "Who gave that to you? Give it here." There's a note stuck to the package with Scotch Tape. She reads the note aloud to Grandpa: "Dear Betty, I want to see my girls. Please call me at Hillside Hotel. Love, Merle."

"Betty is not going to like this," Grandmommy says.

"It's my watch," I say. "It's for my birthday. It's from my darling dad. Give it to me."

Grandmommy won't give me the watch.

I tell the girls at school, "My dad sent me a gold watch. Of course, I don't wear it to school because it's too expensive and it might get lost."

Merle leaned forward. His face was very close to mine. "Did you get the watch?"

The Sadness reached out and wrapped long prickly fingers around my throat, squeezing tight. I couldn't swallow, couldn't speak.

I nodded.

Then Merle talked about something nobody had ever talked about before. "I heard about what Clay did to you," he said, "and when I heard he got off, I went lookin' for him. I went haywire. I wanted to kill him, and the judge, too, for letting him go."

The truth hit hard, battered the child within me...

The Child:

...It's not fair! Clay hurt me. He made me cry. Why didn't the judge put him in jail? Didn't he care?

The Protector:

...Tears rose up, threatening to drown me. My anger erected a dam, over which they couldn't pass. And now I wondered where Clay had gone, afraid some other little girl suffered. Mama had kept me from my dad. He would have protected me from Clay.

I was seven months along when I got called to the Salvation Army payphone. Off balance, I waddled down the hall, like a flat-footed pear on toothpick legs.

"We're getting married," J.D. said into the phone. "I want my kid to have my name."

Now Mama got on the phone. "We'll pick you up tomorrow," she said.

Even though I felt really old sometimes, I was only sixteen. I had to do what Mama said. I wished I was a grown woman and lived in a fine white house and everybody respected me and asked what *I* wanted.

I left the phone dangling, waddled back to my room and lay in the dark staring at the ceiling. From that point on, I had the sense that I had left my body. I floated up near the ceiling. I wondered, Is this what they mean when they speak of out-of-body experience? Astro-travel?

It didn't matter. I liked being able to float and hover above my body.
From that vantage point, I could see myself.
It was like watching a movie, only I was in it.

23

November 1956

I slipped a gray tent with a lace collar over my enormous breasts, down over my big belly. The cheap, shiny fabric stretched taut across my middle and hiked up, leaving the tent several inches higher in front than in back. Lorelei was right. She said I wouldn't wear white on my wedding day. But gray? I covered it with my wine-colored coat. It was old. Worn. I couldn't button it because of my big belly but the color was tolerable.

I sighed, and off we went to the nearest Justice of the Peace.

Mama was wearing a white suit. Ermine collar. Matching fur hat. White suede boots. Silver nails. Orange lipstick. I felt like a squat hen next to a nightingale.

The Justice of the Peace said, "Do you take this man to be your husband?"

I looked at J.D., noticing for the first time that when he breathed in his nostrils flared like a horse, and he had the look of a horse at the gate ready to bolt.

The Justice of the Peace cleared his throat. I ignored him and counted the books on the shelf. two hundred eighteen, two hundred nineteen books on the shelf, three more on the desk. J.D. looked past me at the clock on the wall. Mama glanced at her watch. She gave me a look that said she didn't have all day.

The Justice repeated, "Do you take this man to be your husband?"

I tried to imagine what it would be like to be married to J.D., but I couldn't picture it. *No Sir*, I was thinking, *No Sir, I don't want him.*

Mama glared at me.

I said, "I do."

When it was over, I climbed into the backseat of Mama's Cadillac and scooted over to make room for J.D. But J.D. climbed into the front seat with Mama. She grinned and asked him for a cigarette. J.D. opened Mama's purse, took out a cigarette and placed it between Mama's lips, struck a match, put his face close to Mama's and whispered something. Mama giggled and looked up at J.D.

I wondered, *Am I invisible?* I wanted Mama to look at me. I wanted her to act like a mama should and tell J.D. to get in the backseat where he belonged. She acted like I wasn't even there.

Now Mama stopped at a liquor store to buy VO and a newspaper, and J.D. jumped out and ran after her. Seemed to me like Mama went out of her way to get J.D.'s attention, swinging her butt side to side, wrinkling her nose and giggling.

Ignoring me, Mama and J.D. sat in the front seat, leaned over the *Classifieds,* circling apartments, their heads close together, then Mama drove us around to look at them. One was better than the rest and when I said, "I think it's the best so far," Mama whipped out her checkbook, paid the landlady, and then took off with J.D., leaving me alone on my wedding day.

The apartment was cold. Dark. Musty. Hardly big enough for two. The tiny kitchen had fine old cabinets and a small drop-leaf table just like Grandpa's. A shade hid a tall narrow window. I tugged at the shade. It rolled round and round. Dust flew every which way, dancing in the now sun-filled room. I retreated and leaned against the paneled wall in the parlor, coughing violently. I ran my hand down the mahogany wall. It came away black. This was not at all the home I wanted for my baby.

The Sadness sat on my shoulders and wrapped its scrawny fingers around my forehead and screamed. At the same time, I heard someone cry out. There was a child crying somewhere in the darkness. A long time ago, before I dried up inside, I would've cried myself but not now. Now I held everything in.

The baby shifted, pressing against my bladder. I waddled into a bathroom so small you could stand in the middle of the room, reach out and touch all four walls. I plopped down on the toilet, my knees touching the radiator on the opposite wall, put my head in my hands and retreated into a velvety black place inside my head...

---◆---◆---

..."It'll be all right," I said to myself. "Nobody can make me stay if I don't want to." I looked around the room with a fresh eye. The ceilings were high, and the mahogany paneling was nice. I climbed up on the green velvet sofa and ripped down the ugly drapes, which were covered with gaudy cabbage-size orange flowers, then took down the dingy sheers and threw them in the bathtub to soak. While the curtains soaked, I carried the drapes down to the basement, scrubbed the grimy bay window inside and out, rinsed it with vinegar and dried it with newspaper.

Finding the wood floor in good condition, I rolled up the faded carpet, and struggled to get it down the basement stairs. The woman across the hall heard me wrestling with the rug and poked her head out her door. "Hi," she said, "looks like you need help."

Clarice was a quiet, pale, pinched little thing, like a weed growing through a crack in the pavement, her head covered with pin curl snails, each impaled by a bobby pin. The snails were very black, as if they had been drenched in ink.

When the water in the tub turned the color of a urine sample, I rinsed the snowy sheers, hung them up to dry, washed and waxed the walls, then got down on my knees and scrubbed the floor, removing layers of grime, letting the hardwood grain shine through.

While the floor dried, I sat on the front porch watching a small red-headed woodpecker tapping on the maple tree. The sky was clear, the ground covered with frost. The light was beginning to fade.

Hard to say how long I sat there all goose pimply. Shivering. Ten minutes? An hour? My memory dull, I struggled to remember where I was. I rubbed my hands together to warm them. That's when I saw it. There was a ring on my left hand. My head throbbed. *Where am I? And where did I get the ring?*

My memory was slow coming but after while I remembered I had a husband. Mama had brought me there. I remembered that much.

I went inside. Where I expected my apartment to be was a much nicer one with shiny floors and a wonderful bay window that looked out at the maple-lined street. I walked all around the building, went inside and stood in the entry, confused, unwilling to believe that the apartment Mama rented had disappeared.

Clarice opened the door and stuck her head out. "Are you all right?"

"Not really. I can't find where I live. Mama left me here all alone."

Clarice's head snapped around so that she was looking right at me. She was looking at me real peculiar. "Are you kidding?" she asked. She saw that I wasn't. "Honey," she said softly, "there's only four apartments. Two upstairs. Two down- yours and mine. You're standing right in front of yours. Here, come sit down. You've been working too hard." She took my arm and led me inside.

We sat on a green velvet sofa, which looked vaguely familiar. Everything else looked different. "What happened to the carpet?" I asked.

"*You* happened to it. The place looks fantastic! You really have worked a miracle in here. The floor looks great!"

The apartment *was* nice. And the floor did look great. But I would've sworn I'd never seen it before. I went to the window and looked out. Darkness had fallen on my wedding night. There was a full moon, and the moonlight was shining through the trees, making lacy shadows on the snow. It was near eleven. I went to bed alone.

At ten minutes past midnight J.D. crept in and crawled into bed beside me. Almost immediately he began to snore.

———— ◆ ———— ◆ ————

J.D. and I had been married one month. It was Saturday night. I was sitting propped up in bed embroidering tiny handmade baby clothes, listening to the DJ at the Drive-In Restaurant count down the top 40. Then I heard J.D.'s voice dedicating a song to Elaine. The Disc Jockey asked him how he liked the prom. J.D. said it was bitching. *Prom?* My husband was at the Drive-in dedicating a song to the girl he took to the prom.

The radio now sounded less loud and not so near. I couldn't make out the words. The room was blurry and bitter cold. *The Sadness* was so close I could smell its breath. *The Sadness* opened its cold mouth wide, daring me to jump in so it could swallow me whole. I turned away.

Just before dawn, I woke to loud music coming from a car parked outside the apartment. I looked at the clock. 1:08 a.m. I stumbled, half asleep, to the window and looked out. I saw J.D. with three girls, drinking, and tossing beer cans on the lawn.

He came in an hour later, swaying unsteadily, reeking of whiskey.

"Have a nice time at the Prom?" I asked sarcastically.

"None of your business." Still in his tux, J.D. fell across the bed and slept like a dead man.

I wrapped myself in a blanket, hunkered down on the sofa like a small child, willed myself to disappear and got lost in the black empty space inside my head...

...Next thing I knew I was sitting on the sofa, wrapped in a blanket, reading a story in *True Confessions* about a girl my age that got pregnant and had a thin sickly baby- a little birdlike thing. It died. I lay awake, my hands on my stomach, waiting for my baby to kick. When at last the vigorous little kicks came, I drifted into an uneasy sleep.

I'm walking down the long, white hall of the Salvation Army Hospital. A tiny foot sticks out of my stomach like a pin in a pincushion. By the time I find the nurse, the foot has disappeared. She sends me back to my room. The foot comes back.

I walk down the long hall again, but the foot has vanished. The nurse sends me away. The foot reappears. I walk down the hall again. The hall becomes a bus station. People scurry away. No one will help me. They all have some place to go. The baby is coming! I go behind a white curtain. A doctor is there. I'm in the delivery room. My baby is born but they won't let me see it. A voice squawks, "Birdlike, birdlike, birdlike."

"Let me see my baby," I say. No one hears. I am alone. I climb from my bed and walk down hall to the nursery. There, one crib stands, separated from the others. I am drawn to that lone crib. "My baby. My baby," I whisper.

A voice echoes inside my head, "You'll be sorry, sorry, sorry... birdlike, birdlike, birdlike."

Summoning all my courage, I tiptoe to the tiny crib. A commotion within the crib startles me so that I jump back. A stark, ugly bird flies from the crib and out the open window.

I woke up drenched with sweat. I got up, splashed cold water on my face, then went out and sat on the porch, watching the snow fall.

Clarice found me sitting on the porch shivering. "How long you been out here?"

"I don't know."

Clarice took my hand and led me inside. "Crabs and ice water," she said, setting a plate of brownies between us. "Crabs and ice water, honey, that's what you got when you got J.D."

The brownies were warm, chock full of nuts and gooey in the middle. I dunked one into my tea. The tea was weak, steamy hot and sweet, the way I like it. Outside, the wind blew its frigid breath at snowflakes as they fell, whirling and swirling. Some stuck to the window like ice stars. Clarice's kitchen was warm and snug and smelled of chocolate.

An odd little thing, Clarice read pulp fiction all day, fornicated half the night. Every night. I heard them thumping away. There was never any other sound until the end when she uttered one high pitched little cry. I found it hard to believe she'd been married four times, all four to Eugene. Clarice told me herself, so it must have been true.

"I wish I'd been doing something else when I met J.D.," I said. "He doesn't care about the tiny baby clothes." I wiped a tear from my eye. "He calls me Fatso and stays out late."

"I know. I hear him stagger in all hours of the night. Only the devil knows where he's been or who he's been with. Not a damn thing you can do about it either, with you expecting, any day now."

———————————————

On the day before Valentine's Day J.D. announced he didn't want to be married anymore. We had been married three months. Mama had come to take me home with her.

I clamped my teeth closed. "I don't want to be alone when the baby comes," I said between clenched teeth.

Mama looked up at J.D. and fluttered her eyelashes. "J.D., can't you stay until the baby is born? Do it for me."

J.D. took a pack of Camels from his shirt pocket, lit a cigarette, and took a drag.

I glanced around the empty apartment. My wedding ring still soaked in a glass of ammonia on the kitchen counter. Mama had taught me to clean jewelry that way. I wiped the ring on my blouse, thinking, *it's too bad it doesn't mean anything.* I liked the ring anyway, because Merle bought it for me. I struggled to put it on. My fingers were swollen. I was covered in hives.

J.D. laughed in my face. "What's the matter, Fatso? Can't get your ring on?"

I felt my face flush and my heart started beating out some kind of awkward rhythm. I threw the ring at J.D., stomped across the room and faced him straight on. "You think it's funny?" I asked. "I'll show you something *really* funny." My hand flew through the air and landed hard on J.D.'s cheek. "And I'm *not* fat. I'm *pregnant.*"

J.D. walked out and slammed the door.

24

Los Angeles 1958

I had gone from the frying pan into the fire, as Grandmommy used to say. I hoped things would get better after the baby was born, after J.D. came back. But we moved three more times in six months. J.D. couldn't keep a job. He stayed out all night. Slept half the day. Sometimes, in his sleep, he called out, "Audrey."

It was the middle of the night and I was fast asleep. J.D. shook me awake. "Get up and fix me something to eat," he demanded.

"What's the matter with you? I'm eight months pregnant."

"You lazy shitass bitch!" J.D. grabbed me by the arm and drug me from bed, knocking me to the floor. "Lazy bitch, I'll go eat where I'm welcome." J.D. stumbled out the door.

"Good riddance," I mumbled under my breath.

Afraid of what J.D. might do when he got back, I gathered seventeen-month-old Danny in my arms, wrapped him in a blanket and slipped into the hot, humid night.

As I walked along the dark deserted street, I felt myself rise up out of my body. The first time I had left my body and looked down at myself, I was afraid. Now it happened often enough that it didn't scare me anymore. Separated from myself I could observe all that went on but feel nothing. I watched myself walk in slow motion down the empty street.

It was 4 a.m. Danny was heavy. My legs hurt. Back ached. I came to a car parked in a driveway. I tried the door. Locked. Walked on. Station wagon. Unlocked. I slept sitting up, the baby in my arms, until the chill of the night woke me. I climbed out of the station wagon, stiff and weary, and walked slowly back home.

J.D. was passed out on the bed. I undressed and stood under the shower, soaping a purple bruise on my thigh. Sharp cramps radiated from my back to my belly. They came and went with alarming requency. The hot shower calmed me, soothed my sore, aching body. The water turned from hot to warm to cold. I stayed in the shower until the pains subsided, then wrapped my swollen body in my faded blue and threadbare robe.

I took three aspirin. Boiled water. Added salt. Stirred the oats. Danny banged his spoon against the highchair. I sighed. Another day had begun.

Merle's ship was in, and he stopped by for a visit. "Where's J.D.?"

"Down at the corner. At the bar."

Merle headed out the door. He came back holding J.D. by the scruff of the neck. He dragged him over to the bassinet. "Is this your son?"

"Yeah. So what?"

"Well, you're damn well going to support him." Then Merle, I mean my dad, took J.D. down to the Merchant Marine Union Hall, called in a favor and put J.D. on a ship headed for Japan.

I wondered, *How will we survive on $3 until my allotment check comes?*

It was August. The sidewalks were blistering hot. Danny had no shoes. I waddled down the street carrying Danny, eighteen months old, on my hips, his head resting on my big belly. Across the street, less than two blocks away was a small market. It seemed much farther in the sweltering heat.

Once inside the market, I leaned against the counter, letting the small fan on the counter cool my sweat-soaked body. I bought baloney and bread, baby food, milk, and a grape Popsicle for Danny, then trudged back to the motel, groceries in one arm, Danny in the other. He sucked contentedly on the Popsicle, his lips turning purple.

I poured the last of the milk into Danny's bottle, fed him the last jar of baby food and tucked him into bed, then checked the cupboard one more time, hoping I had overlooked something to eat. Damn. Cockroaches. Contemptuous of the light, the roaches slunk into dark shadowy corners. My heart beat a cockeyed beat against my ribs.

I lay down and tried to sleep. My stomach wouldn't cooperate. For three days, twice a day, I had eaten one slice of baloney between two slices of bread. Now there was nothing left to eat. My stomach grumbled fiercely, and I thought about J.D. with one leg shorter than the other on account of his mother had nothing to eat but potatoes when she was pregnant. I thought about the baby growing inside me and me with no food now for 28 hours, and I thought about all that food in the little market down the street.

I got up and wrote a note on a piece of brown paper bag, folded and torn neatly:

Dear Grocer,
I don't have any money.
My baby needs milk and baby food.
I'm pregnant. I need to eat, too.
I'll write down everything I take and
when I get my allotment check I'll pay
you back.
Yours truly,
Lucinda

It was dark now and Danny was sound asleep. I slipped into the night, headed for the market. I walked down the empty street, the echo of my footsteps the only sound. Now I heard my heart beat, louder and louder, faster and faster. My face was hot. I knew it had turned red. I was ashamed, ashamed I had no food for my babies, Danny and the one waiting to be born, and ashamed because of how I was going to get it.

When I reached the market, I glanced up and down the empty street. Seeing no one, I crept around behind the store and tried the door. Locked. Near the dumpster was an empty milk crate. I turned it upside down beneath the window, thinking I could use it for a step stool. If the window was unlocked I could climb in.

"What are you doing?" a deep voice asked gruffly. I turned to face a cop silhouette six foot four, a blinding light coming from his right hand. "Are you trying to break in?"

"Yes." My voice had gone squeaky. "I'm hungry."

"You wouldn't do that," the cop said, his voice gentle. "You're a nice girl."

"I'm not either. I got pregnant before I got married and now I'm pregnant again. My husband doesn't love me, and I don't have any food for my baby."

"Let me see what you've got in your hand."

I looked down at my hand. My fist was tightly closed. I still had the note.

The cop put the sweaty, blurred note in his pocket, then drove me home. He was looking through my cupboards when the police radio squawked. "I have to go now," he said, "I'll deal with you later. Do not, and I mean do *not* leave this house!"

I waited for the cop to return, wondering what it would be like in jail. *Do they have baby food and milk in jail? Or will they give Danny bread and water, same as me?* It never occurred to me that they wouldn't let me keep him. I fell asleep propped up in bed, facing the door.

At half past midnight, a loud pounding at the door woke me. A blue light flashed outside my window. "Open up. Police," the cop said in a deep gruff voice. He had come for me. I thought about running but there was only the one door. I couldn't run. I thought about hiding but I knew I couldn't get my big belly under the bed. There was nowhere to hide. I tried to swallow my fear but it got caught in my throat. My breath came in ragged spurts.

"Open the door!" He pounded again, louder. "Police!"

I opened the door a crack.

"You got anybody close by?" I shook my head. He handed me a dime "You call your mother first thing in the morning, or I'll come back and put you in jail. Do you understand?"

I nodded. He handed me a paper bag. In it a hamburger. Fries. Milk shake. Milk for the baby. Four jars of baby food.

I called Mama first thing. She called Uncle Edward who was living nearby, and he took me in.

Less than a week had gone by when Mama called. "Merle's dead," she said into Uncle Edward's phone.

"Merle? My dad? Dead?"

"Drowned in a bathtub in a two-bit hotel. Drunk, as usual."

"Drowned?"

"Some say he had a heart attack, some say he passed out, slumped down in the tub and drowned. I think he got in with the wrong people, owed some money, and they killed him."

I hung up, went out the door and walked away from the sadness. I was walking fast, thinking about my dad. If only he hadn't drowned, he might have quit drinking. I had never seen him take a drink, not even one. But sometimes, after he'd been to visit, I'd find a bottle stuck down behind the couch cushion or under the chair, and once I couldn't flush the toilet because there were two bottles in the tank.

If only my dad hadn't drowned, he might have quit drinking and moved into one of those pretty houses on a lovely street lined with maple trees and I could have visited him. We could have made up for all those lost years. But he didn't quit drinking. He died, abandoning me again. I was thinking about all that and walking fast, with tears running down my face, when a sharp pain tore across my belly.

----◆----◆----

They put me in a ward at Los Angeles County Hospital with nineteen other women, some on the verge of delivering, like me, and some with newborn babies attached to their breasts.

I named my baby Steven. He turned towards me instinctively, rooting like a piglet, clamping down on my breast, sucking impatiently. Larger than the next largest in the nursery by a pound, his cry, louder and deeper than the other babies, was easy to distinguish. I was very proud. "How on earth will she manage with two babies only eighteen months apart," they said.

Knowing I could depend on no one but myself, I wrapped my hospital gown tightly around my soft little belly, marched down the hall and asked to use the phone.

The nurse said, "You cannot use this phone."

----◆----◆----

The Protector:
...Anger simmered in the midst of my belly, boiled over, ran red hot through my veins and into my mouth. "Who do you think you're talking to?" I reached over the counter, wrestled the phone from the nurse, called the Union Hall and arranged to have my allotment check brought to the hospital.

I rented a dreary one-room concrete-block cabin with an asphalt yard. The concrete walls inside and out were painted the color of baby shit. A naked light bulb hung from a frayed wire. There was a metal bed, a chest of drawers, a small table and two chairs painted dark high-gloss brown. In one corner, a tiny stove, a small refrigerator, and a sink made up the kitchen. In another corner, a thin partition closed off the shower and toilet. Across the third corner someone had attached a pole from which hung a dozen wire hangers. I hung up all my clothes, leaving eight empty hangers. All I owned in this world, besides the clothes, was a highchair and the wicker bassinet I had lugged from place to place.

Two weeks passed and still no word from J.D.

"When will the ship arrive? I said into the phone.

The man on the ship said, "We've been here three days. This Audrey?"

I hung up.

———————◆————————

When J.D. finally decided to come home, he expected me to be glad to see him.

"How's Audrey?" I asked sarcastically.

"None of your damn business."

"Bastard," I said under my breath. I had never sworn before, and never thought about what affect it might have on J.D. His reaction was swift. He came at me, his face twisted, his blue eyes icy slits full of hate. Now he sucked in air, blew it out his mouth, like a locomotive building up steam and charged. I stood rigid, my arms at my sides. Even when I saw the fist coming towards me I didn't flinch. The fist slammed into my nose. My head wobbled and fell forward. My teeth clanked together. Dazed, I turned away. Tears stung my eyes.

Without saying a word J.D. stomped out, slamming the door as he left.

I walked stiffly across the room and peered into the mirror. My nose was broader, flatter, wider. There were blue-black smudges beneath my eyes. Bloody snot trickled out one nostril and ran into the corner of my mouth. I ran to the toilet and puked.

The next day, J.D. dumped me off at a trailer park and took off for India. Once again, I found myself in an unfamiliar place with no memory of how I got there. For me, there were no teary good-byes and exchanging of telephone numbers when I moved. I had no friendships built up over the years. I was isolated, scared, and broke. I was thinking, *I can't depend on J.D. I need to get myself a job. But what? I'm a high school dropout. Who would hire me?*

The hot California sun beat down on the tin box we called home. The ramshackle trailer was cramped. Airless. Hot. While other girls were at the beach with their boyfriends, I sat and sweated with two cranky babies, both covered with prickly heat rash.

Danny, not yet two, played outside the trailer door, dust clinging to his sweaty little body. Stevie, two months old, cried, miserable in the heat. I picked him up and carried him to the washroom. Danny toddled along behind. I stepped into a concrete shower stall painted battleship gray and turned on the shower, dipping first the baby, then Danny, under the stingy drizzle of water the color of weak tea. It smelled of chlorine.

Someone had left the *Los Angeles Times* Want Ads behind. I picked up the paper and tucked it under my arm. While the boys slept, I poured over the classifieds, finally circling:

INSTRUCTORS WANTED
Apply
VIC TANNY GYMS
Beverly Hills

Determined to get the job, I talked the manager of the trailer park into watching the boys, promising to pay her with my first paycheck and hitchhiked to Beverly Hills.

Vic Tanny's was swarming with good-looking men and women dressed like movie stars. The receptionist, a synthetic blonde with silicon breasts and false eyelashes, frowned when she saw me. I was wearing shorts, a T shirt and rubber thongs.

"If you're interested in a job you'd better go home and change," she said.

"I don't have anything else to wear," I mumbled. The receptionist ignored me. I straightened my shoulders. "I'd like an application please."

"They don't need anybody else."

Just then, a platinum blonde, wearing a lavender miniskirt, asked for an application and the receptionist gave it to her.

The Protector:
"Excuse me," I said, leaning over until my face was not more than three inches from the receptionist. "I want an application."

She hardened her face. "Just a minute." She got up out her seat and left the room, her matching plastic breasts leading the way.

When she came back, she had the boss with her. He was six-foot four, his hair blonde and long, like the mane of a lion. He was golden-brown with a thick neck and shoulders so wide he had to turn sideways to get through the door. He grinned, flexed his bulging biceps, and stood so close I could see yellow flecks in eyes the color of topaz. And a new side of me surfaced...

The Body:
...Actually, it wasn't a new side but one that had been repressed for over four years. I was now *The Body*, the one who had danced so provocatively in high school, the one who wanted to be Marilyn Monroe. I looked up at the boss and smiled appreciatively.

"Is there a problem?" he asked.

"No problem. I want a job and she won't give me an application."

"It's hard work."

"I don't care how hard it is. I need this job." I was practically begging. "I'll show up every day and I won't be late. I can do the job."

"Stay. Take the test. If you pass, you're in."

The other applicants stared at the way I was dressed. A few snickered but laughed out the other side of their mouths when *The Student* got the highest mark.

After that, *The Body* got good paying jobs managing gyms, posing for pin-up magazines, and go go dancing.

I felt like I had already lived a lifetime of trouble.

I was eighteen years old.

25

And now I will tell you what happened that caused other memories to surface... Thirty years had gone by. There were marriages. Divorces. I had five children. I moved around. I went from job to job, trying to find something that would take away the sadness.

Massachusetts 1977

"The foliage is beautiful this year," they said. "Don't get much prettier."

The Sadness pointed out dead leaves rotting on the ground.

I was walking down Main Street when, out of the corner of my eye, I caught a glimpse of a woman reflected in the window glass. She wore a frumpy coat that was missing a button or two and buttoned cock-eyed. Her dress was too long. It hung down three inches below the coat. The old woman shuffled along beside me, walking all stooped over, weighted down by despair and hopelessness. I cringed. I wondered how many shattered dreams it takes to beat down a woman, bend her, break her. I turned to speak to her.

The old woman had vanished.

I crossed Elm Street, and then, as I passed by the bank, I saw the old woman again. I stopped and whirled on my heels to face her.

The tired old woman I saw in the glass was *me*!

I walked home slowly, trying to make sense of what I had seen in the window. In the privacy of my own bathroom, I stood before the mirror and stared at the listless face that stared back at me. Yellow-gray skin. Stringy matted hair. I was shocked to see the toll life had extracted from me.

I looked into the dull brown eyes and tried to stir up something inside myself but there was nothing there to jostle. I felt already dead, like the dead, dry leaves that fall onto the path where they are trampled, bruised, and ground into the dirt.

I crawled into bed with *The Sadness* and lay staring into blackness, feeling nothing. As the night crept along, I tried to imagine myself in another life. But what? I tried to will myself to *feel* something. Anything. I sank my fingernails into the softness of my arm, pinching as hard as I could. Hot, salty tears sprung up from some place deep within me and ran down my cheeks. I was much relieved to feel pain after so long a time of not feeling anything at all. Towards morning, I fell asleep curled up in a ball, hugging my knees to my breast…

…The sun burst forth, lighting up the crisp October morning. My head still ached and the ringing in my ears hadn't left. I forced myself to rise, took a deep breath and faced the new day feeling odd and unsettled, as if I had been away.

I stood on the porch and watched the leaves fall from the trees. They fluttered to the ground where they lay huddled together in a dull, lifeless heap. Life had been cruel, had knocked me down and trampled me.

I saw a leaf caught up by the wind, carried higher and higher. That lone leaf soared out of sight and with it came the courage to try again.

The woman I saw in the mirror was thirty-seven. Kind brown eyes looked back at me, giving me courage to begin anew. I could see right off, I needed to fix myself up.

My kitchen became a beauty parlor. I saturated my hair with warm olive oil, wrapped my head in a towel-turban and slathered my face with an oatmeal mask. While the mask dried, tinted my nails a soft rose. The mask dry, I scrubbed it off, my face now fresh and clear. I showered, shaved my legs, washed my hair, and took painstaking care putting on my makeup.

I was good at reinventing myself.

I pasted on what I hoped was a confident smile and went out and got myself a job at a brokerage firm- Merrill Lynch, Pierce, Fenner & Smith.

———◆—————◆———

My hotel suite was fifteen minutes from the World Trade Center, where my firm's offices were located. Every day, when I came up out of the subway, I wondered, *Do those people down there know this is up here?* I imagined a whole city of people who had never seen the light of day, who scurried here and there in the dark passageways like so many rats. Every day the pack of people scurried through the subway maze, depositing their shiny tokens, as they had been taught. They were rewarded by the opening of the gates. I wanted to yell, "Stop! You don't have to do this. You are people. People!" They wouldn't have listened to me any more than I listened to the man in the subway who warned me that the world would end at three o'clock.

In the subway I felt superior. In the World Trade Center, I felt inferior, an impostor. My firm had brought the cream of the crop from all across the country to train together. At first, I felt out of place, afraid that any minute they might discover that I was not as bright as the others. Yet every day I seemed to myself more like the others.

I didn't go home on weekends. I was afraid that if I went home I might not know who I was.

I stared into the mirror in my hotel room. The eyes staring back at me were not *my* eyes. I had changed. I had taken the best of me and become somebody else.

In New York City I had become *The Stockbroker*.

———————————◆————————————

My date and I sat near the window, watching the tide come in. The restaurant was built on the wharf. A thick gray mist came up behind the wharf, creeping around and over the dock. I watched the fog swirl all about, and when the fog cleared, I saw a lighthouse. In my mind flashed another lighthouse. *Lighthouse. Fog. The mournful sound of a foghorn warning of danger.*

"I used to live by a lighthouse," I said.

"Where was that?"

"I don't know."

"You don't know where you lived?"

"We traveled a lot. I don't remember where it was." The fog covered the lighthouse. I could still see the other one in my mind. I could still hear it crying in the night.

"I think I'm going crazy," I said.

My date looked at me as if he thought it might be so. "Really?" he asked, "Why is that?"

"Sometimes, when I least expect it, something will flash into my mind. I remember things. Bits and pieces. Fragments of my life pass through my mind. Sometimes the memories hit me like an incoming wave, flooding my mind, threatening to drown me."

"What do you remember?"

"A lighthouse blinking in the fog. Stairs. I couldn't go up and I couldn't go down," I blurted out, realizing I wasn't making any sense. I lifted my drink and pressed the cold glass against my throbbing forehead. "I can't remember where the lighthouse is. Maybe I'll go back someday *if* I can remember where the lighthouse is. If I can remember, I think I'll go back. Someday."

He looked at me strangely. "How was your childhood?"

"Real good," I said. I thought I was telling the truth.

26

As *The Stockbroker* I made more money than I ever expected, doubling my income two and a half times in two years, and earning trips to England, Denmark, Holland, Belgium, and Italy. I wore silk. Cashmere. Real leather shoes. Mink. Gold.

It was then that odd things started to happen. There were bruises on my body, and I didn't know how they got there. One day the children heard me fall. By the time they got to me, I was already standing and didn't even know I'd fallen.

The doctor said, "That explains the bruises. You've been blacking out. We don't know why." Now I think it was just a way of postponing the memories.

They came anyway...

I was sitting in my car waiting for the light to change when a long-lost memory surfaced:

The Child:

…I'm a little girl. Angel and I are sitting in a parked car with Clay while Mama shops. I'm not sure what town we're in, maybe Bremerton. On my right is a big store. General Mercantile. Montgomery Ward. Maybe JC Penny's. Angel and I are in the back seat playing "I Spy." Angel does everything I say, even if I don't say I spy. Clay gets out of the car. "I'll be right back," he says. Now Clay jumps into the car, acting peculiar, holding the steering wheel so tight his knuckles turn white, looking in the rear-view mirror, turning to peer over his shoulder. I hear somebody screaming way too loud. I cover my ears but I can't block out the terrible sound of a baby hurt bad. Sirens. Police cars were suddenly parked every which way, and right in the middle of the street. Blue lights flashing. Police are holding back a lady. She's screaming something awful. She tries to get to the car that's parked right behind us but the police won't let her. Screaming ambulance pulls up next to the car. Policeman hands over something. Or somebody.

Mama pushes her way through the crowd that has appeared from nowhere. "Oh, my God," she says as she climbs in the car, "somebody raped an eighteen-month-old baby girl in the car parked right behind us. They left her for just a minute. Oh, my God."

I hear Mama say somebody raped the baby girl. Maybe that's the word I need to tell about Clay bothering little girls. Now, people push up against the right side of our car. On our left is a policeman, not more than three feet away. I reach for the door handle. "Let me out. Let me see. Let me see the police. Let me see the little girl."

"You stay real still," Clay says. Yellow eyes warn, you better not know too much.

Better not know too much! "I heard a little girl screaming and want to get out and give her a cookie," I say. The lie satisfies Clay.

I tell Angel, "Simon says put your finger up your nose."

Mama says, "Don't be so silly."

I'm so silly. I don't know nuthin'.

Now other memories surfaced. They came to me in bits and pieces. Fragments. I remembered things I hadn't known but when the memories came, I knew I had always known. The memories were there all along, in the shadow of my mind, keeping me from myself. When I remembered, there was no beginning and no end, and the middle was all jumbled. I dreaded the memories. I never knew when they'd come, forcing the visions upon me.

A month went by. I sat on the bed already dressed for work. I bent over to put on my shoes and my mind flooded with images. It was as if I was watching a picture show in the back of my head, except that I was *in* the movie:

...I'm a little girl. I'm in a car watching the windshield wipers work furiously, useless against the rain. It's raining like a cow peein' on a flat rock. Mama says, "Take the ferry, it'll be quicker". The wind blows on the water, agitating it, making choppy waves. We take the long way. On my left, at the side of the road, a pink EAT sign glows in the dark and rainy night. A man stumbles out of the bar and starts across the road.

Clay yells, "Asshole!" The car hits the man and knocks him down.

"Stop the car!" Mama screams, "Stop the car!".

Clay stops the car and gets out. I'm sitting in the front seat in Mama's lap, wrapped in a blanket like a tiny baby, a bulky blood-soaked towel between my legs. In the rear-view mirror, I see Clay turn the man over, take his wallet, push him over the side of the road, then come back to the car. He tells Mama. "He's all right. Just drunk."

As I relived the memory, my heart thundered in my chest. I broke out in a sweat. My chest rose and fell in ragged shallow breaths. I was astonished to have forgotten something so vivid upon remembering. As the memory took hold, a voice inside my head asked gently, *Where were you going?* I struggled to remember. *Rain. Windshield wiper. Ferry. Blood.* The memory tumbled out and flooded my mind. I remembered the doctor's office:

"Someone has been fooling around with her," the doctor says. "Having dealt with matters like this before, I can tell you that little girls are funny about it. They won't tell but someone has been fooling around with her."

Mama stares straight ahead. Seems like she don't hear the doctor. Poor little Mama.

When we get home, Mama puts Angel and me in her bed and goes downstairs.

I hear yelling and cussing. Mama comes running upstairs with a fist full of knives in her left hand, a hammer in her right. She drags the chest of drawers across the room, pushes it up against the door, jerks Angel up out of bed and puts her on my lap. Angel wakes up howling.

Mama manages to wedge the bed between the chest and the wall, barricading the door before Clay rattles the doorknob and rams the door. It won't budge.

"Betty, let me in."

"Get away from the door."

"Let me in. I love you."

"You get away from the door."

Clay pounds his fists against the door. "Open the damn door!"

"Get away from the door. I'm warning you."

Clay pounds harder.

Mama sticks the longest and sharpest of the knives in the crack of the door, so that only the handle shows, then slides it up and down the edge of the door.

"Crazy bitch," Clay mumbles to himself.

"I told you to get away from the door."

"Okay. Whatever you want. I love you. I'm going." We hear Clay's footsteps on the stairs, then the front door slam. Mama sticks the other three knives in the crack.

"What are you doing, Mama?"

"Just in case."

Mama lies down on top of the covers, fully dressed, with the hammer in her hand. Angel and I wrap our arms around each other and rock ourselves to sleep.

I sat on the bed breathing fast, sucking the oxygen out of the room.

"*And before that?*" prompted the gentle voice inside my head.

My head ached. I did not want to remember but the memories kept coming. There was no way to stop them. In slow motion I relived a night long ago:

...It's sometime after midnight. The child I used to be wakes up...climbs out of bed...stands gazing out the window. Night has fallen all around her, and in the dark, a mysterious gray cloud hovers at sea level. The sea is black, smooth as glass, like obsidian. The night is dark and somber, with no moon shining. There are no stars. There is only the phosphorescent glow of the lighthouse's yellow blinking light.

The silence of the night is broken by the long sorrowful sound of the foghorn crying out. Turning away from the window, the scared little girl stares into the blackness. Straining her senses, she makes out the sound of hushed, shuffled footsteps coming up the stairs. In the darkness she sees a frightful shadowy figure in the shape of a man. She jumps into bed and pulls the covers up over her head.

In a drunken stupor, Clay sways and staggers as he slowly makes his way towards the child...he drags her out of bed...throws her in Mama's bed...he's drunk...he's tearing her nightgown...she jumps off the bed and crawls under it...he grabs her ankle...drags her out from under the bed...he hits her with his fist and tries to put his stinking whiskey tongue in her mouth...she keep her lips closed tight...he sits on her and pushes something terrible in her mouth.

She vomits.

"*I need a drink of water,*" *she says.*

She runs downstairs to get the butcher knife she hid under the stairs.

It was gone!

Clay grabs her arm. She slips from his grasp and runs up the stairs. She trips and falls, then sits hunched up on the stairs, clinging to the banister, her terror-struck face wet with tears.

Clay says, Come back downstairs do you hear me? You come back here.

She doesn't hear what he says. Focused on a fly caught in a spider web suspended from one stair rail to another, she concentrates on the desperate buzzing sound the fly makes, until there is nothing inside her head except the droning of the fly, which grows louder and louder until the monotonous buzz becomes one sound like a Buddhist mantra.

Clay claws at her arm. She pulls away and runs upstairs. No use. Clay is right behind her. She starts back down the stairs. She can't go down. She can't go up. Clay grabs her. She struggles to free herself from his grasp.

She knows she cannot escape. She hums to herself, as if she is one with the droning, buzzing fly. Her senses numbed, Clay's voice sounds far away and she can barely smell his whiskey breath as he pushes her to the floor and holds her down. Beads of perspiration form on Clay's forehead. Drops of sweat rain down upon the girl's small naked body but she is unaware of her nakedness and no longer feels his weight. She hides in that still black place inside her head. Velvet blackness rises up and wraps itself around her fragile mind and shields her pain.

She hears someone else cry out.

Afterwards, when Clay speaks to her, she doesn't answer. Unaware of Clay's presence, she pulls herself to her feet, stumbles, then straightens up and walks naked to her room, her face pale and streaked with tears, her dark, hollow eyes staring straight ahead, her legs stiff and straight like a toy soldier. The child climbs the stairs and gets into bed and sinks into a black abyss, oblivious to the blood.

And I knew then that she and I were the same.

"Clay!" I screamed, "You sonofabitch! How dare you!"

I threw one shoe against the closet door, the other against the wall. All the while, I watched myself from somewhere up near the ceiling. I grabbed the pillows from the bed. Strangled them. Beat them. Threw them to the floor. Jumped on them. Ripped the covers from the bed. Knocked the lamp off the bedside table.

I seized the porcelain doll on my dresser by the neck and squeezed. The head fell off and rolled silently across the floor. My hands were sweating. I looked down. Now wet with sweat, the red velvet dress had stained my hands. *Blood!*

In one sweeping blow I cleared the dressing table. Perfume, photo and hairbrush toppled and fell to the floor.

I yanked down the curtains. The curtain rod hung by one small nail. I grabbed the rod and wrestled it from the nail, twisted it into a shapeless, mangled mass, and threw it at the wall. "You dirty, good for nothing, low-down spineless coward," I screamed, "I'll strangle you with my bare hands. I'm not helpless now, you sonofabitch!"

For twenty-two days I stayed in my pajamas. I didn't bathe or comb my hair. I sat by the fire and gazed into the flames, obsessed with the memories. There were dark empty spaces in my memory. There was darkness everywhere I searched, and everywhere were tight-lipped can't remember people who thought they knew what was best for me. The devil was breathing down my neck, prompting me to let the secrets lie.

As I relived the terror, I dreamed up ways to kill Clay Stout. Nights were spent in uneasy slumber as I plotted the perfect murder and, even in the light of day, I tried to perfect the scheme. Suppose I shot him, and he didn't die? Suppose I tried to shoot him, and he shot me? Suppose I tried to poison him, and someone else ate the tainted food?

I killed Clayton Stout a thousand times. But he would not die.

EWanda M. Cheney

San Diego, 1985

Except for the polio she had as a child, Mama hadn't been sick a day of her life. Now that she was, the whole family rushed to her side.

Mama wore blue jeans, flip-flops and a green and white striped knit shirt. No earrings. Her lips were pale. Mama's hair was very short. Gray. Mama had *gray* hair. "Oh, you cut your hair," I said. "It's cute."

Mama shrugged. "Angel had it cut. In case it falls out, you know. It won't. I'm a witch. I witched it *not* to fall out, you know."

Choosing not to argue with Mama, I turned away, glancing around the room. Mama's apartment was small, sleek and modern, in shades of off-white, the monochromatic scheme broken only by the purple orchids growing on the windowsill. On the chrome and glass coffee table there was another orchid, this one white, and a medical journal. "Where'd you get that doctor book," I said.

"I swiped from the doctor's office."

"Mama!"

"I wanted to know how bad it is," she said. "I'm gonna take it back." She flicked her cigarette lighter. The flame flared up and reflected in her eyes. Now pale green, they told me she was scared.

Hot, humid air pressed down on us, making it hard to breathe. It was late September. Back home, in New England, the leaves were crimson and gold, the air cool and crisp. Here in San Diego, it was near one hundred degrees. I was sweating. My blouse was soaked and the hair on back of my neck wringing wet.

"Jeepers, it's hot." Uncle Edward said. He hadn't changed. His hair was still black but for a touch of gray above his ears. His eyes were gentle, his face full of goodness.

Patsy looked the same. Years of trusting the Lord had given her the unlined bright shiny face of a Pentecostal lady unfettered by worry, believing that no matter what, God has a plan.

"They're *both* preachers now," Gwen said. "Patsy's gone from preacher's daughter to preacher's wife. Now she's a preacher in her own right. Pentecostal preachers. They raised eight kids, some Gospel singers like themselves. Grandmommy would have been proud."

I nodded.

In the time it takes a hummingbird to flit from one flower to the next, thirty years had flown by. Everything had changed. Nothing had changed. We had only grown older.

"Bones is in the kitchen," Mama said. "Does she know you're here?"

Aunt Bony was standing, her back to me, leaning into the counter, her shoulders hunched, making a salad large enough to feed a whole tribe. Face flushed, hair cut short like a boy, eyes bright, she wore boy's boy's jeans and a knit shirt. She was barefoot, her toenails painted the color of blackberries. I tapped her on the shoulder. "Hey, lady, I'm hungry," I said. "Know where I can get something to eat?"

Aunt Bony turned around. With half a tomato in one hand, a paring knife in the other, she threw her arms around me. I smelled whiskey on her breath. "You little skunk," she said in that deep familiar drawl. "Gee whiz, what're we gonna do?" She blinked rapidly. The tears came anyway.

Now the door burst open and a large, vivid woman dressed in a red floral printed dress bounced in. With that hair, even blacker than it used to be, in a knot on top her head, her skin paler than ever, a slash of vibrant red on her lips and those green eyes, Aunt Alberta looked like a three hundred pound powdered and painted geisha." She giggled. "Lucinda, it's me- your fat but nice Aunt. I've been sober now for over fifteen years. I traded alcohol for sweets and gained two hundred pounds."

Mama grinned.

"I used to be what they call a periodic drinker," Aunt Alberta explained. "I used to disappear for months, years at a time. When I got tired of it, I joined AA, married Lew and moved to Arizona. Never drank another drop. Fifteen years, three months, eighteen days. Sober."

"That's great. How'd you do it?"

"I wanted children. Couldn't have any of my own, so when Eddie and Patsy adopted those little Indian girls, I got clean. I take in orphaned children until they are adopted. They keep in touch. I have twelve now. If you want what you've never had, you must do what you've never done before."

"That's wonderful."

"Amen," Patsy and Uncle Edward said at the same time.

"She's a big," Aunt Bony added. "She speaks at AA meetings all across the map." Aunt Alberta blushed. "Ralph quit drinkin' before I did."

Uncle Ralph stood up and stretched. "I saw myself on Angel's home movie, actin' the fool. Stumblin' like a drunkin' sailor. I was mortified. Never took another drink."

Mama took a long puff and blew cigarette rings into our faces, obviously bored with the conversation.

Aunt Alberta changed the subject. "Betty, don't you worry about a thing. I'm gonna clean your whole apartment. I'll stay as long as you need." From the oversized canvas tote she had brought with her, she took a rag and began dusting Mama's piano, stopping every few minutes to pop candy into her mouth.

I sat, without moving, and looked around the room. It looked to me like the set for a play. The good family gathered to be with their sister in her time of trouble. All we needed was music. The whole family was musical. They could have doubled as actors, orchestra and choir.

Although I was there, surrounded by a loving family, I felt apart. It seemed I was always apart from the others. Sometimes, up near the ceiling. I was an observer. On the outside. No one knew, of course. Had they known, they would have gathered me in their arms and told me how much they loved me. I was loved. I knew that. But I didn't feel it. Fact is, I didn't feel anything. Some thought I was aloof. Lucky for me, my family saw it as sophistication.

Nevertheless, I was happy to see them.

A few minutes later Angel and Zoe arrived. Zoe was carrying two large buckets of chicken and a brown paper bag, which she took directly to the kitchen. Mama grinned when she saw the bag.

"Doggone it," Angel said, handing Mama a dozen lavender roses, "Dontcha want your flowers?"

Mama giggled. "Oh, aren't they beautiful. Hey, they match your dress. Look, Alberta, Angel brought me roses. Aren't they gorgeous?"

Aunt Alberta nodded. "Bones, did you see the roses?"

Aunt Bony studied the roses carefully. "Well, I'll be damned," she said.

"What *beautiful* roses," I said, "What kind are they?"

"I don't know," Mama said, "but they sure are pretty."

We kept on that way, talking about the roses. We needed something to distract us from the business at hand. Cancer, Death's right hand, had come for the great Betty.

----◆————◆————

Like strangers, we sat in awkward silence in a semi-circle around Mama and stared at her. Mama sat like a queen holding court, drinking VO straight, in a tall glass, and smoking cigarettes in a long silver cigarette holder, held as if it were the queen's scepter. We pretended we didn't see her bottom lip quiver, and when she reached up to wipe away tears, we looked away.

Angel fiddled with the roses. Uncle Ralph looked at the floor. Aunt Alberta filled a bucket with hot water, got down on her knees and scrubbed the bathroom floor. Uncle Edward turned gilt edged pages of his Bible. "Betty, the Bible says in Jeremiah, "I will restore your health, and I will heal your wounds, declares the Lord." He put down the Bible, "God can heal you if you ask him."

Mama stared at Uncle Edward through squinted eyes. "I've got my own religion, you know. I don't need the Bible. And I don't pray. I just witch what I want. And I get it."

Uncle Edward looked at Patsy, like he thought Mama just be headed straight to hell. Patsy closed her eyes and said a silent prayer.

The kitchen timer buzzed. Patsy jumped up, ran into the kitchen and took golden brown biscuits out of the oven.

"Ralph," Mama said, "Look at Patsy's biscuits."

Uncle Ralph cocked his head and put his hand to his ear.

Uncle Edward said loudly, "Betty said 'Look at Patsy's biscuits'."

"Oh, I thought she said Patsy was taking fits." Uncle Ralph jumped up, jerking his body. He staggered across the room, still twitching. When he got to the biscuits, he took one in his left hand and held it up, "Look," he said, "after Patsy's fit, she made biscuits." Aunt Bony chuckled. "Shoot, Ralph, you can still tickle my funny bone."

Uncle Ralph put the biscuit down. "The funny bone's connected to the hip bone," he sang. "The hip bone's connected to the leg bone, the leg bone's connected to the-" He pointed in mock horror to Aunt Bony's bare feet. "*Big* toe." We all laughed.

"Bones, do your flat foot dance," Uncle Edward said, and Aunt Bony, urged on by her brothers, stomped and shuffled her bare feet against the floor, making slapping sounds like a slow motion tap dancer with no shoes. Before long she got tickled at herself and got to laughing so hard she couldn't go on. The awkwardness had disappeared.

"Doggone it. Let's eat," Angel said, putting a drumstick and a biscuit dripping with butter on a plate for Mama. "Mama, you want salad dressing?"

"Sure. Honey, bring me my cigarettes. Wonder where Matt is."

———————————

"Well, gee whiz, you look like some kind of wizard," Aunt Bony said. And he did. Black eyes. Long white hair. Close to seventy, Uncle Matt had grown a-foot-long beard. A self-proclaimed guru, he wore a long purple robe. Sandals. Never one to mince words, he got right to the point, "Betty, what did the doctor say?"

"Cancer. Lung cancer."

"Will you have chemotherapy?"

"Already did."

Aunt Bony gulped. "Well, gee whiz, Betty, will the chemo cure it?"

"Not if it's already spread." Mama's mouth flopped over on one side. She stuck her chin out, took a long puff on a cigarette and went into a coughing fit. We watched helplessly as violent convulsions racked Mama's body. She coughed like that for a long time, whooping and shuddering, gasping for breath.

Uncle Ralph took the cigarette out of his mouth and snuffed it out in Mama's silver ashtray.

Aunt Bony stopped puffing on hers, held it under the faucet, then threw it into the trash. "Gee whiz, Betty, when will you know?"

The coughing over, Mama continued hoarsely, "Three days. Then I'll know if I'm a goner." Mama lit up another cigarette, took a drag and started coughing again.

"Doggone it, Mama," Angel said, "Doctors aren't always right."

"Angel's right," I said, "Doctors don't know everything."

"Doctor's don't know *anything*," Uncle Matt said. We all nodded our heads in agreement.

"I know it." Mama took a drink. "Besides, I'm a witch. I can beat it. And I won't lose my hair, you know. I witched myself not to get sick from the chemo, and I can witch my hair not to fall out."

Now Aunt Alberta came in from the patio. She had cleaned the smoke-tinged sliding glass doors inside and out. Her face was flushed, her hair damp. She wiped her forehead. "Betty, can I use your phone?"

"What for?" Mama was annoyed. She wouldn't give up center stage easily.

"I want to call Roy and see if he's coming. He should've been here by now."

"I'll call."

What happened next is hard to believe. I swear it's true. Mama dialed Uncle Roy's number. "Ethel? It's Betty." Mama paused. "I'm all right. You know me. I'm tough. Let me talk to Roy." We heard only Mama's side of the conversation. "When?" Mama's eyebrow shot up. "What happened?" Speechless, Mama listened to what Ethel had to say, placed the receiver back on its cradle, then turned to us with a blank expression. "Roy's dead."

Uncle Ralph cocked his head and put his hand to his ear. "What'd she say? Roy's in bed?"

Uncle Matt said loudly, "Dead. Roy's dead."

Aunt Bony swallowed hard. "Gee whiz, Betty, what happened?" Although she was the tallest one on the room, she suddenly seemed very small. She blinked her big brown eyes and wiped away tears. "What happened?" she repeated.

Mama's cigarette had turned to ash. She flicked it onto the floor and tossed the filter into the ashtray. "Ethel said Roy was writing a letter to me, you know. He wrote that if he could, he'd let Death take him instead of me. They found him at his desk, the letter half finished, you know, the pen still in his hand. Dead."

Aunt Alberta was standing in the middle of the room, facing Mama. "Roy? "Roy? My brother Roy?"

Mama was too choked up to answer.

Aunt Alberta was twirling round and round, shaking her hands like she just burned them on a hot stove, hopping up and down, making sounds like a hurt puppy. A lock of hair escaped from the bun on top of her head and fell into her eyes. "Ooh, ooh, ooh," she cried over and over.

Angel jabbed me in the rib. Teary eyed, lower lip quivering, she whispered, "Aunt Alberta and Uncle Roy always were close. I feel bad for Alberta. I don't remember Uncle Roy. I haven't seen him since he denounced 'the whole damn family,' said we were all possessed by demons, and went to live in the desert."

"Well, people who fall off roofs and land on their heads do things like that sometimes," I whispered back.

Aunt Bony hadn't moved. Her eyes were open wide, like a frightened animal caught in the headlights of a speeding car.

Aunt Alberta was still twirling. "Ooh! Ooh! Ooh!" she cried.

Mama looked to her oldest brother as if to say, "Can't you do something?"

Uncle Matt jumped to his feet. "Roy's not dead," he said. His voice was loud and quivered just a little. His eyes were wild. He waved his arms like a zealous prophet. "Roy's spirit has gone to a better place. His spirit has joined the universal spirit of truth, and the universal truth is everywhere, even here, and Roy is here with us now, and he's not dead, he's now a part of the universe, part of the great universal truth, and the great universal truth is *universal*!"

We all stared at Uncle Matt, as if he had said something profound. The truth is, Uncle Matt had gotten involved with crystals and pyramids. And he smoked stuff.

Uncle Matt jumped up and down. "Don't you see, Betty? You don't have to die. Roy died so you don't have to."

"Bless his heart," Mama said. You could see she believed Uncle Roy had died in her place.

For three days Mama sat next to the phone, waiting for the doctor to call. She scarcely ate. She hardly slept. She didn't change her clothes.

Three days later, when the phone rang, we waited helplessly. Patsy held Uncle Edward's hand. Aunt Alberta stopped scrubbing. Aunt Bony's eyes darted around the room, like she didn't know where to look. Matt took a crystal out of his pocket and rubbed it between his thumb and forefinger. Angel crossed her fingers. Uncle Ralph looked at the ceiling. Zoe hid in the kitchen. I held my breath.

Mama put down the phone. We waited, not knowing what was coming next.

"I'm not dying," Mama said. "Not yet." She held up her glass. "I'll drink to that." She emptied the glass. "See, I told you. I'm a witch. I witched the cancer away, you know. And my hair didn't fall out."

"Praise the Lord," Uncle Edward said. "Thank you for this healing. In the name of Jesus Patsy bowed her head. Aunt Bony wiped tears from her eyes. Uncle Matt kissed the crystal. Uncle Ralph picked up Mama's ashtray and took it into the kitchen. Angel and I followed him, pretending we needed a drink of water. Zoe ran cold water and splashed her tear streaked face.

A few days later, when Mama brushed her hair and it all came out in her hairbrush, she cried out like a banshee betrayed by a spell gone wrong.

28

Brimfield, Massachusetts 1987

It's strange how things change, how one thing can change everything. And that is what happened next... One evening, I went with a friend to a cocktail party. Somebody brought up a woman in the news who claimed that she had suddenly remembered that her father had killed a woman years before. The woman had been a child when it happened. She had repressed the memory for many years.

Some didn't believe her. They didn't believe memories could be repressed, and then suddenly be remembered. That's when I admitted that I had repressed memories of my own. As it turned out, one of the guests at the party was a producer on the Sally Jesse Raphael Show. She asked me to appear on a show about repressed memory. I went and told my story.

The calls that came after the show validated my memories:

Angel: "Do you remember us going to visit Clay when he went to jail for the hit and run? Remember? Mama left us outside playing and we could look down and see the jail.

"I remember a brown building with barbwire all around it," I said. *Angel is playing in the dirt. I'm looking down the hill at a big brown building. There's a high barbwire fence all around. Pee runs down my leg, leaving a wet spot in the sand.*

"Doggone it, that was the jail. Clay did time there for the hit and run. Remember when he took the wallet and pushed the drunk over the side of the road?"

"I didn't know you were in the car."

"I was in the back seat. I was jealous because you were sitting on Mama's lap. I didn't know what had happened." She paused. "Did Clay ever go to jail for what he did to you?"

"No. He was let loose. I was the one thrown into the black hole."

Aunt Bony: "Well, you little skunk, I'm proud of you. Gee whiz, Sally Jesse Raphael. I wish we could've protected you from that bastard. Pervert. Remember when he reached into the backseat and grabbed my titty, and I socked him? Remember? Mama slapped him and Papa almost killed him? Remember? Too bad he didn't die then."

"Yes. Yes. I remember. Castle Rock. I thought maybe it was just a bad dream."

"No, it was real."

Then neither of us said anything for what seemed like a long time.

Aunt Bony broke the silence. "We tried," Her voice faltered. "We tried to protect you. We told Betty to watch out for Clay." I could tell she was crying. "Why didn't she listen?"

"She didn't know."

"But..." Aunt Bony was sobbing now and couldn't go on. She hung up.

I breathed a sigh of relief. I felt like I had spent my life buried under a dung hill, and now, shovel by shovel, the shit was being removed. Still, I knew there was an important piece missing. Something buried so deep I couldn't retrieve it.

--- ◆ ---

Aunt Alberta: "Can you let it go now? Now that you talked about it, can you let it go?"

"Not yet."

"I was raped. Did you know that?"

I wasn't sure I should tell her I knew. "I think I heard something about it," I said.

"I held it all in for years and damn near drank myself to death before I told." Aunt Alberta's voice was tinged with sadness.

"I'm sorry," I said. I wished we could reach through the phone and wrap our arms around one another and have a good cry.

And then, she told me the whole story, which I will tell you at a later time.

"I'm better now," she said, so that I wouldn't worry. We knew we would never speak of it again.

"I'm glad."

"Let it go."

"I can't. There are still gaps in my memory, things I can't remember. I'm like an unfinished jig-saw puzzle. I have to put the pieces together."

Aunt Alberta sighed.

"I want a copy of the court transcript. I want to know what happened."

"Don't you remember?"

"I remember the D.A. asked, 'Do you know Clayton Stout? Is he in this room?' And there he was, sitting at a table with his lawyer. I couldn't understand why they let such a bad man sit there, instead of in jail. And when the D.A. asked me what happened on the night of

December 20, 1948, I didn't know which night they meant. There had been so many nights. I wanted to get it right. I could see Clay's evil yellow eyes, his grinning, leering smirk. I was scared. I hollered, 'Judge, Sir, I wanna go home. Clay's looking at me.' They took me to the library. I need to know what happened while I was out of the courtroom."

"Why not just forget about it and get on with your life? You might find out something you don't want to know."

"I *need* to know."

"Well, then. Try the courthouse at Port Gamble."

Mama: "I saw the show." My heart beat a little faster, and I kind of held my breath, waiting to see what Mama had to say.

"Your hair looked good," she said.

"Thanks." I was waiting for her to say something about what I said on national television about being raped when I was seven years old. I was waiting for her to say something about Clay Stout.

"Your dress was perfect. You can tell you're the daughter of the *great* Betty."

She hung up.

After the call, I went out and sat on the front steps, watching the sun set. I watched it drop lower and lower until it disappeared behind some trees. I was thinking, I finally have a place to start. Port Gamble.

Before long, it was dark, and I could see the moon peeking through the maples, making mottled patterns on the ground. An owl called into the night.

I was thinking about all the things I had remembered. I knew there were other things still buried in my subconscious. I was filled with dread, scared of what I might remember next.

Three weeks later, the court transcript arrived. My hands shook as I opened the documents. According to the record, what I remembered was right, except I had the date wrong. Even after I saw it written down, official, it seemed to me like there was a whole year missing and I wondered what could've happened to make a small child black out a whole year.

The record did not contain a transcript of the actual court proceeding but there was a copy of a letter Clay had written to Mama:

My Darling,

I'm so lonesome and messed up I don't know what to do. I can't very well advise you what to do because it is me that is wrong you can't realize how I feel. I can't believe it is you and I and my little family that are separated. I can't sleep or eat. I go to work in a dream. I got knocked off the rig Monday. I just couldn't think fast enough to step out of the way.

Do the kids talk about me any? What did Grandpa think of the little stove? That man that was hit at four corners, you know, Livenston I guess is about to die internal injuries the Deputy Sheriff and State cops was out last nite and questioned me until 10:30. I think they are satisfied I hope asked where you were and I told them you had gone to visit your folks over Christmas.

Darling if ever a man was punished I am it I am living through hell and torment of my own making. I'd like nothing better than to have the right to tell you to bring your mother, Dad and both kids and come on home. I know you can never forgive me for if you could you would be bigger than God himself. I am satisfied in my mind and heart that the other Clay is dead and this one don't have much desire to live.

I have the strangest feeling that I'll never see you again. I don't know why. I've prayed for you and the children yes and for myself too. I wish you were up here so you could have time to

*think things out about it and I could see that you didn't get hungry
while doing it. Tell your folks hello for me.*

    *I got a payment book on the vacuum cleaner today they
finished it will take care of it Friday.*

    All my love

    Clay

"Can you believe the bastard was still lying to Mama, still trying to
manipulate her after what he did," I said out loud to myself. "Trying
to make her feel sorry for him. Did he really think she was that stupid?

    Like a tornado, torturous memories whirled inside my mind. My
head ached. My heart beat erratically. But I knew I must keep searching
for the final piece to the puzzle of my own life.

DIVORCED WANT TO OPEN COCKTAIL LOUNGE WILL YOU RUN IT FOR ME?

Prompted by the telegram from Bill, Mama packed her fancy gowns and Zoe's frilly little dresses and moved back to Valdez. When Mama got off the plane, she walked straight into Bill's arms.

Mama and Sox got divorced and sold the house in Oregon, leaving Grandmommy and Grandpa without a place to live. Aunt Bony and Glen took them to Albuquerque, and they moved into the small house behind the big adobe house where Aunt Bony and Glen had lived for thirty years.

I visited often. They were happy there. Aunt Bony's four strong sons made sure Grandpa didn't have to work too hard in his garden.

Yet, Grandpa had always loved the woods. When we bought a piece of land and built a house in the country, I wanted him to come to New England to see my trees. Maple. Oak. Fir. I wanted Grandmommy to walk with me through the Lady Slippers that grew beneath towering white pines. "Grandpa," I said into the phone. "Come for a visit. I'll send you plane tickets. Or I can drive out to get you and we can drive back together. Whatever you want."

"We're too old," Grandpa said. We can't be gallivanting halfway cross country."

"Well, if you change your mind, let me know. Meanwhile, I'm going to send you some photos. And leaves from my trees."

"That's a fine idea," he said.

And so, I collected leaves from every bush and tree and pressed them with a hot iron between sheets of waxed paper. I pressed wildflowers for Grandmommy. I looked up the proper names and painstakingly labeled each page in gold calligraphy. I took photos of Lady Slippers, bird's nests, woodpeckers, and the barred owl that lived in the pine tree behind the house. The books were nearly finished.

Then, towards the end of winter, I got the worst phone call I had ever gotten.

Albuquerque, New Mexico 1975

At the funeral hall, Grandpa lay still and quiet on white satin, dressed in his best suit. Angel reached into her pocket, took out manicure scissors and snipped off a lock of Grandpa's hair. She put it between the pages of a small book and slipped it into her purse.

Grandmommy leaned over Grandpa's coffin. "Albert, oh, Albert," she said in a small voice. She whispered a private prayer, stepped back, raised her hand, the one with the handkerchief and waved. "Adios," she said. It was the only time I ever heard her speak Spanish.

That night Grandmommy crawled into bed dressed in her best nightgown, lay with her arms folded across her bosom and prayed, "Sweet Jesus, take me home."

I was sitting by the fireplace, leafing through the *New Yorker* when the bad news call came. "It's me. Bones. Mama, Mama, she's — gone. The doctor said she died of a broken heart. It took her less than two months to convince Jesus to take her before her time so she could be with Papa."

"Ohhhh," was all I could say.

"They were eighty-five years old. They had been married sixty-eight years."

I looked around for some place to hide. Seeing none, I hid in the dark place inside myself...

..."Why did they have to die?" I wailed.

The scrapbook I was making for them was finally finished. "Stupid scrapbook," I screamed. I ripped the pages to pieces, ripped the pieces into pieces, then ran outside into the ink-black night. I grabbed a baby tree, a small pine, pulled it up by the roots and ripped off the branches. Intent on tearing up every single tree, I moved on to the next and the next. The Sadness tripped me. I fell in the blackness and lay face down on the bruised moss and sobbed. I cried out to God. Shook my fist. Yelled impiously, "You had no right to take Grandmommy and Grandpa. I hate you, God! Do you hear me? I hate you! Give them back!"

God's breath filled the black empty night. Then God spoke, his voice thunderous, rolling across the sky. I couldn't make out what he said. Lightning flashed. The rain came. "Are you crying, God? Are you sorry? Or are you trying to drown me?"

I whispered, "Grandpa. Grandmommy. I miss you."

30

Brimfield, Massachusetts 1986

Abrand-new silver van pulled into the driveway. It was Mama. My heart skipped a beat. The muscles at the base of my skull tightened. I hoped she wouldn't stay long.

Mama climbed out and leaned against the van with her butt stuck out. She wore snug blue jeans and an orange shirt with a green cactus embroidered on her left breast. A cowboy hat hid most of her hair, which was now pinkish orange. It didn't hide the long, dangly earrings. "I look pretty good for an ole bag, don't I?" she said, twirling around so I could admire her. "The doctor declared me cancer free. I'm cured, cured with medicine made from mold in a cave in Italy. I ought to be cured. My pills were $300 a piece. They wrote me up in the medical books, you know."

I was shocked at how Mama had aged but told her she looked great.

"How do you like my van?" Mama slid open the door. "It's customized, you know." The van had four plush swivel seats, two little round tables, mood lights, a freezer, a sink and built-in slots for Mama's crystal whiskey decanters. "If it wasn't for my van, I'd be homeless. You don't mind if I move in, do you?"

I gave up my study to make room for Mama, and she moved in with me.

I was forty-six years old now, and most of the pieces of the puzzle were in place when it appeared without warning. A precipitous fragmented memory in the back of my mind, a long lost memory precariously teetering on the brink of recognition. I was driving to work when it happened. Teeth. Paw. Tail. No shape. No form. Imperceptible. A shadowy flicker. Gone. The hair on the back of my neck bristled.

Three days later, with half an eye I saw it again. A black shadow in the shape of a dog.

Then I didn't see hide nor hair of it for days. It lurked just out of sight, a dim shadowy dog-like beast. From between its teeth, a low guttural sound poured like hot piss into my ear.

"Remember?" it growled, "Remember?"

I did not.

I had not seen the beast's face and did not recognize it, and now I became obsessed with knowing its name. If only I could remember, I thought the mysterious creature might provide the final piece of the puzzle.

I was driving along the highway when the beast appeared again, much clearer now. It was black and brown. A large flop-eared dog. A cur had crept inside my head. It was very hot. I was feeling faint. I pulled the car over to the side of the road. The dog stayed with me. So, we drove home, the dog and I, and that night as my family gathered for dinner, I could talk of nothing else.

"What's with the dog?" they said, "Enough about the dog."

There it was again, that ineradicable flicker at the edge of my mind. This time it came so close that my hand flew to my forehead, as if I could brush it away.

Mama's eyes narrowed. She took a puff off her cigarette and blew smoke in my face. "Now what's your problem?" she asked, like I'd given her nothing but trouble my whole life.

"It's nothing."

"You look like you've seen a ghost."

"It's the dog. I keep seeing it."

"Where?" She started towards the window.

"It's in my mind. The first time I didn't know what it was. It just flashed into my mind. It's a dog. Black with tan paws. A big dog."

"You smoking? Are you on drugs?"

"No. No. Nothing like that. It's like when you have a word on the tip of your tongue. It's like that, only it's on the edge of my mind."

Mama rolled her eyes.

"Well, huh," I said, "That's odd."

"What?"

"The dog. I saw it again."

"Get me some coffee."

———————————◆—◆———————————

Mama was late getting back from her senior group gig. Barely able to stand, she leaned against the wall so she wouldn't tip over. She was wearing a gold metallic T-shirt down to her ankles. On her feet were gold see-through plastic high-heeled shoes. In her hand that damned silver cigarette holder I had come to despise. "You shoulda sheard me play," she said, slurring her words. "I wow'd 'em."

"I bet you did."

"No, really. You really, really shoulda sheard me play. I wow'd 'em. I really, really wow'd 'em. I'm shill the *great* Betty."

"I know it."

"No, really. You don't know. I'm the *great* Betty, you know, I shill got it." Mama was staring at nothing, wobbling, hanging on to the wall.

"Sit down before you fall down," I ordered.

Mama sat down next to me on the sofa, grabbed hold my arm and dug in her nails. "If I got myshelf a shittle place on a lake, wouldya, couldya maybe vishit me? I mean, wouldya maybe jes maybe vishit me shometime if I got myshelf a place on the lake, 'cause I could get me a shittle place on the lake."

"Yeah, I'd visit you. Why? Don't you like it here?"

"No, I mean if I got me a place on the lake, wouldya, you know, wouldya vishit sometimes?"

"Mama, you know I would."

"No, I mean really, really wouldya, couldya jes drive all the way over to the lake an' vishit your poor ole mama? I mean, like if I wasn't playin' a gig, you know, wouldya vishit me?"

"Mama, you're drunk."

"Well, sure, I might've had a few but you don't know, you don't unnershan'. I'm the *great* Betty. You don't care, you jes don't care." Mama leaned forward. I felt her hot stinking booze breath on my face.

I closed my eyes and tried to escape to the black place. But this time I could not escape.

Mama bombarded me with drunk talk, cutting me down, shrinking me until I was a child...

... *The Child* had no choice but to stay and be assaulted by the slurred repeated words that made no sense. She tried to pull away but Mama had hold her arm. Her eyes filled with tears. She swallowed. The tears went down salty...

...Oddly, I changed again. I was much stronger. I could protect my inner child. I got up and took the child that lived inside my head and walked away.

Mama no longer had any power over me. She must have realized it, because, as soon as she sobered up, she tossed her clothes into her old tan suitcase. "I'm going to visit Bones," she said. She climbed into her cocktail lounge on wheels and drove into the blinding sun.

————————◆◆————◆————◆————

"Bones had been drinking off and on all day," Mama said when she called. "You'd think she'd learn. She was sitting on the floor in her bedroom, drinking out of the bottle, sloshing vodka all over herself. By the time she finished the bottle, she was soaked pretty good. She had a cigarette in one hand and a lighter in the other. She put the cigarette in her mouth and, with an unsteady hand, held the lighter to the cigarette, flicked it once, twice. On the third try, it flickered and lit. She brought it to her mouth, sucked in air and puffed on the cigarette, forgetting about the lighter. The vodka ignited. Her eyelashes were singed, then gone. Her eyebrows disappeared. Her sweater caught fire, then her hair burst into flame."

"Oh, my God."

"I heard the blood-curdling scream. I ran into the room and saw my baby sister on fire, the cigarette still hanging out her blistered mouth, the lighter still in her hand. Breathing in the odor of scorched flesh, I grabbed the blanket off the bed, flung it over her and threw her to the floor, rolling her over and over to smother the flames."

"Oh, my God. Is she going to be okay?"

"One third of her body is charred." She'll have scars."

Aunt Bony said she was grateful to be alive, insisted she'd never take another drink.

"Bones is a changed woman," they said. "Something happened that day, something besides the fire. Something Bones saw. Bones wouldn't say."

Mama told everybody, "I think Bones saw something." In later telling, Mama said, "Bones saw something that scared her. Who knows, maybe the devil." Before a week had gone by, Mama was saying, "Bones saw the devil himself, standing in the flames, beckoning to her."

Mama had always been a storyteller. Fact is- the whole family told stories. Most of them true. Sometimes the truth got stretched. Trouble is- if you stretch the truth far enough, it'll snap back and hit you in the face.

Aunt Bony didn't drink after the fire.

Not for a whole year.

After Aunt Bony's accident, I found myself thinking a lot about the past. I was thinking about how Aunt Bony had been like a mother to me, and I was thinking about that damn dog that sometimes flashed into my mind.

The dog beast haunted me. Yet still the creature had no name. No face. He was so close I could feel his breath. He crept closer and closer. Now I was surrounded with the smell of him. He crept stealthily through foggy memory and then leapt swiftly into my conscious mind. Shifting, vaporous mist evaporated. My mind broke open like a ripe watermelon whacked with an axe. Memories spilled out. I could see clearly through the haze. Its eyes burn into mine. It seems less fearsome now, more like a playful puppy. The dog is licking my face. Jack. My dog Jack. A mongrel pup.

It struck me as very odd to be thinking of Jack over forty years later, but I could not let that fragmented image go. The impulse to chase Jack's ghost image was too strong. Old Jack held some secret- a missing piece to the puzzle of my past.

I remembered: *Jack doesn't come home one day and I go looking for him. On the third day I find him. He had been hit by a car and thrown through the basement window of a nearby church, his right front paw badly cut. I carry him home to the old house in Trinidad, where I'm in third grade. Mama takes a needle and thread and puts twelve stitches in Jack's leg.*

I remembered when we first got Jack. *We're driving across country. Angel and I were sleeping in the back seat. We wake up. We're parked in front of a diner. We get out of the car, go inside, climb up on stools next to Mama, and order chicken fried steak. As we leave, an abandoned black and tan puppy follows me to the car. I open the door...the puppy climbs inside...Mama lets me take him in the car with us to...Trinidad, Colorado.*

Once the memory tumbled out, I knew I must have it wrong. *Angel and me in the back seat, snugly nestled against down pillows. Warm. Covered with a Grandmommy-quilt, a warm puppy between us, our arms wrapped around him...Mama sitting in the passenger seat, smoking, the window cracked.* I held my breath and closed my eyes. I wanted to run, run away from the memories. I had spent my life searching for answers, and now I did not want to know. I did not want to see who sat in the driver's seat.

But I had come too far.

My mind rotated, memories tumbling, rearranging themselves, resting first on one image and then another, like a kaleidoscope. *Mama sitting in the passenger seat. And now I see the driver. A man. A man in a checkered shirt.* His image burned itself into my brain. I went over and over all that I remembered, and it all fit together neatly. That is, except for the fact that I got Jack in 1948. Clay was there, in that car, when I got the dog.

Mama had gone back to Clay after...

The memory, now grown powerful, lunged at me, hit me hard in the chest. It was hellish to remember. I saw the puzzle now complete, the pieces fit. All these years, I had thought that when Mama found Clay out that bleak December night in 1947, I had thought she did the right thing. I had never blamed Mama. Now I knew. I wanted to grab hold Mama and shake her until her body went limp and her teeth rattled in her head like pebbles in an empty tin can.

Now I knew the truth.

31

I thought that once Clayton Stout quit invading my mind, once my repressed memories had been found out and pieced together, I thought that I would be at peace.

I was not.

I was still tormented. But why? The Sadness sat on my shoulders and wrapped its scrawny fingers around my forehead, squeezed and hissed, "What about Mama?"

I had unfinished business with Mama.

Portland, Oregon 1988

Mama sat propped up in bed, wearing a green hospital gown. Face pale. Eyes closed. Hair very short, no longer red. Mama had *gray* hair. Gray! Angel turned to me, her eyes open wide. I knew what she was thinking. *We're too late.*

"Mama," I said, not expecting an answer. "Mama."

To our surprise, Mama opened her eyes. "You're here. I was afraid I was gonna die alone."

Angel stared at her feet. I counted the squares in the ceiling.

"We wouldn't," Angel stammered, "we wouldn't leave you alone."

"Well, what do you think?" Mama placed her hand on her chest.

"What?" I asked, thinking maybe she was pointing out how thin she was. She weighed only eighty-six pounds.

"My gown. What do you think?"

"What?"

"My gown," Mama said impatiently, "They knew I couldn't have an ordinary ole hospital gown. I'm the *great* Betty, you know, so they had mine special made."

"Oh," Angel said, "It's real nice."

Mama turned to me. "Don't you see? It's green, like my eyes. Have you ever seen one like it before?"

"No," I lied, "it looks good."

"I'm gonna beat this thing."

"I know it," I said, not very convincingly.

"I really am. I'm a witch, you know. I'm gonna beat this thing," Mama said, smoothing down her gown. "Honey, bring me my purse." Mama rummaged through her purse, found a half pack of cigarettes, took one out and lit it. She took a puff, blew a smoke ring into the air, took another puff, inhaled deeply, took a coughing fit and spit blood into a towel.

"Gosh, darn it, Mama, you're not supposed to be smoking." Angel took the cigarette and flushed it down the toilet.

Mama smoothed down her green hospital johnny, as if it were the most elegant gown in the world. "I am the *great* Betty, aren't I? I really did make something out of myself, didn't I?"

"Yes, you did. You are *the great Betty*," I said.

Mama opened her silver flask and took a sip. "I'll drink to that."

"We're releasing your mother," the doctor said. "Nothing more we can do for her here.

"Releasing her?" Angel asked. She was as surprised as I was. "Today?"

"She can't take care of herself," I said. "She can't live alone."

"No. She can't." The doctor turned and walked away.

"I'd take her home with me," Angel said, "But my apartment's so small you have to stand up to pee. I only have two bedrooms. The kids got rooms, but I sleep on the sofa. I can't take her. I don't have room. Do you?"

"Let's sleep on it. We can figure it out tomorrow. Right now, let's take her to her apartment. Uncle Ralph and Uncle Edward are supposed to meet us there in an hour."

What was I to do? Go back home and leave Mama alone? Stay and lose my job? Take her with me? She had betrayed me. I didn't owe her anything.

We took Mama to her new apartment, wondering, *What will we do with her?*

Uncles Edward and Uncle Ralph arrived shortly after we did, with sleeping bags and extra blankets. We slept on the floor.

The night was interminable. I slept fitfully. I woke at a quarter past six with acid in my gut. Having slept in my panties and bra, I wrapped my blanket around me and walked like a zombie to Mama's tiny bathroom, slipped into my dress, then sat on the floor near Mama, my back against the wall, concentrated on keeping the contents of my stomach where they belonged. I watched Mama sleep. She was no bigger than a child. She couldn't be left alone. Mama was demanding. She wouldn't settle in quietly, gratefully. She'd be difficult. And we all knew it. I choked back a tear. She hadn't been the best of mothers, but she was *my* mother.

Mama woke up at half past eight, stretched and reached for her cigarettes.

Uncle Ralph came out of the kitchen wearing an apron and a chef's hat made from newspaper. He carried a plate stacked high with golden brown pancakes and presented them as if he were a waiter at the Ritz. "I have made zee best pancakes in zee whole world," he announced.

Mama said, "Hey, I could get used to this."

"Betty," Uncle Ralph said, "I've got plenty of room. My kids are grown. Why don't you come live with us?"

"Well, doggone it, Mama," Angel said, "You'd be a fool to turn down an offer like that."

Uncle Edward put his hand on Mama's arm. "Betty, Ralph doesn't live far. You could travel by car."

A wave of relief washed over me. I was off the hook, as they say.

After breakfast we found ourselves alone, Mama and me, while the others stood outside on the balcony smoking cigarettes. Although it was mid-June and warm, Mama had a shawl pulled tightly around her thin shoulders. She reached for a cigarette and fumbled for her lighter. Unable to find it, she struck a match. The flame of the match accented the lines in her face. There weren't many. The ones that were there did not flatter. Mama was an old woman. *When did it happen?*

"Lucinda," Mama said. "Why don't you just say you hate me for what happened. When you were little. You know. Clay. Then maybe you could, can't you forgive me?"

There was ice in my veins and it seemed like my teeth were glued together. "I don't blame you," I said. It was not one of my better lies. It hung suspended in the air and translated itself: I blame you.

Mama stuck out her bottom lip. The left side of her mouth drooped, giving her whole face a crooked, lopsided look. When I saw her like that something hit me smack dab in the middle of my heart. Just like when a baby wrinkles up its little face and looks so pitiful, and you just have to pick it up and comfort it. I walked over and hugged Mama- something I hadn't done before. She felt stiff and bony like a bag of spareribs. She didn't hug back.

I turned and walked away. "I'm going for a walk."

My feet moved as if some mad beast was behind me. My heart beat wildly. My vision blurred. My face wet, I walked quickly, practically running, away from that place, away from that time, but I could not get away from Mama. As I walked past the church, the Sunday service just beginning, a pretty red-haired woman, wearing an orange dress and dangly earrings, passed by. She smiled. And I saw Mama's crooked grin.

Then as I passed the liquor store, a woman stepped in front of me. "Could ya, do ya think ya could buy a gal a drink?" I shook my head. The woman plopped down under the Budweiser sign and lit a cigarette. In her eyes I saw Mama's demon.

Beyond, on the right, a graveyard, gravediggers at work. One leaned on his shovel. He nodded, as if we had business together. I turned away.

I walked back slowly. As I passed the church, I heard a piano playing. *I see Mama's hands lovingly caressing the keys. I see Mama's head thrown back. She laughs a throaty laugh. I see Mama and me, sitting close together in the little red REO, singing You are my sunshine. Mama's picking hops, her back hurting. Mama's tickling Angel and me, making us giggle. Mama's brushing Zoe's red curls and smoothing down her frilly little dress. Mama's mouth is crooked. She's trying not to cry.*

Mama hadn't done right by me. She had always been unreliable. She taught me more about alcoholism than I ever wanted to know. She betrayed me time and time again. She had abandoned me when I was a helpless, innocent child.

Now Mama was helpless as a child, and I didn't have it in me to abandon her.

Worcester, Massachusetts 1988

There was a thunderstorm the day Mama came to live with me. Thunder grumbled like an angry old man. Black clouds rolled across the darkening sky, lit briefly by jagged light. Mama was scared. You could see it in her eyes. I brought her coffee. She asked for tea.

I thought my bringing Mama home to live with me would win me some sort of approval. Maybe some respect. I was naive. Mama seemed happy. But when the phone rang, she answered it in a dull flat voice, complained to Aunt Alberta about the food and told Aunt Bony she wished she hadn't come. Mama complained constantly. She had me running up and down the stairs. The tea was too hot. Too cold. Too sweet. Not sweet enough. And when she sent me after tea and "accidentally" fell on the man I was dating, and I found her with her gown hiked up around her thighs, I knew she hadn't changed.

In July, Mama started taking several naps a day but when she was awake, she told me things, piecing together the fragments of her life. "I worked really hard, you know," she said. "We came through the depression and the war with nothing. I knew the only way out was with my music. I practiced the piano every single day until my fingers ached."

Mama reached for a cigarette. "I was young. Scared. But I worked hard, you know, to become somebody, and then even when I was somebody, men didn't treat me right." She held her head a little bit higher and shrugged like it didn't make any difference.

"I was somebody, you know. I was the *great* Betty." Mama took a puff, inhaled, made a face like you'd make if you bit into sour pickle, and put out the cigarette. "Did I ever tell you that John Wayne used to come into the club in Portland where I worked? The last time I saw him, I was at the piano and John Wayne leaned over and told me I was the best piece of ass he ever had. He said it into the mike so everybody heard."

"I hoped you slapped his face," I said.

Mama was stunned. She had confided in me and I didn't understand. "Don't you see? It was in the papers that we had an affair. It did wonders for business. People came from all over to see me. And he knew, he knew what it would do for my career." She smiled at the memory.

"Did you really sleep with John Wayne?"

"I would've." She snapped her fingers to show how quickly she would have, "But I didn't get the chance."

"Well, I'll bet he wanted to," I said to make up for what I'd said before.

Mama grinned.

Now the grin left. Mama's face crumpled. "I'm dying," she said.

"You're not dying *today*, Mama." I patted her hand. "When you feel better we'll go shopping. I always wanted to go shopping and out to lunch with you."

We both knew we'd never get the chance.

Mama yelled, "Lucinda, come quick." I put two of Mama's favorite cookies on the tea tray and hurried upstairs. Mama was propped up, with her reading glasses on. "You've got to see this." She waved a catalog in my face. "Just look at this. If this isn't you, I don't know what is. Look!" She pointed to an expensive creamy-white silk dress with a matching jacket. "Oh, you've got to get it. It's perfect."

"It's nice," I said. "Classy."

"Mama looked at me in a way I had never seen before. "*You* are real classy," she said. "I like how you dress and I like the way you do your makeup. I've always been real proud of you."

"You have?"

"Well, sure. You're my daughter. I'm very proud, you know. Jealous."

If it hadn't been for that one last word I'd have known Mama was lying.

When the classy off-white dress and matching jacket arrived in the mail, Mama insisted I model it for her. "Let me see." She reached out and felt the fabric. Her hands were thin, white and crisscrossed with spidery blue lines.

"Silk." Mama nodded approvingly. "It's perfect, except for one thing. Honey, hand me my purse." Mama opened her purse and took out a small black velvet bag with a golden drawstring, dumped the contents into her hand and held up her gold nugget bracelet. The one I had coveted for as long as I can remember. "Put it on. I want you to have it."

I held out my arm, admiring the delicate dangling charms through teary eyes, too choked up to speak. I felt like a fine lady, wearing that mess of gold, and, for the first time in my life, I felt like Mama loved me.

I told everybody Mama had picked out the off-white silk outfit. I had myself convinced we'd gone shopping together, Mama and me. I was pretty sure we'd stopped for lunch.

By October Mama had changed so much you wouldn't have believed that she was ever the great Betty. Her hair was sparse and had turned white. She was thin as a child. She talked less now, and when she did there was no hard edge to her voice. Mama smiled the lopsided smile of a shy child. She lived in bed now, rising only to walk slowly to the bathroom. She sat, propped up, leaning against the pillows, wrapped in the afghan Aunt Alberta had crocheted. It was July, hot and humid, but Mama was always cold.

It was twilight, and the first frost-tinged day of the year, when Mama went into a coma. The wind raced and charged about, tossing dry leaves into the air and dropping them. A gray pall covered the ground.

Mama had always been afraid of dying alone so for three days and nights I sat by her side, staring at the tiny shadow of herself that she had become, thinking of all that transpired between us and in the end I did not hate her. She was my mama. I loved her.

I took her hand, not knowing whether or not she could hear me. "Well, I guess we did the best we could," I said gently.

Then Mama was gone.

32

Nearly a year had gone by. I had gone back to college and got my degree. Husband number five had become an all too familiar lump lying next to me in my bed. What once quickened my heart caused me to feign sleep. There is no better way to kill desire than to put a man and woman in the same bed, night after night after night. And, at the end of the day, seat them across from one another where they can watch each other chew. Swallow. Belch. That's enough to snuff out passion that begins red hot like molten lava, slides downhill from there, then cools, leaving you with a black lump where your heart is supposed to be. A marriage gone bad is like that.

To get away, I went to San Diego to visit Angel. That night, I lay on the sofa, beneath the large painting of Elvis on velvet, unable to sleep because Angel insisted that the television be left on. "Angel," I said, "Why can't you sleep without the television?" Angel rummaged through her purse, took out a pack of cigarettes and lit one. "Why can't you sleep without the television on?" I repeated.

Angel took a puff and blew out the smoke. "Well, shit, it's because, you know, because of what that pervert did to me? I'm fifty years old and I'm still afraid of the dark."

"What pervert?"

"Clay."

"Clay?" I couldn't believe my own ears. "Clay? Did he? Did he?"

Angel nodded.

Although the room was cool and a breeze wafted through the window, I felt very warm. I tried to protect you," I said. My voice was very small. I had failed. I closed my eyes. *I see Angel, innocent as a chubby little cherub, fluffy blonde hair bright as a halo. Big eyes. Smiling. "Me do somersault," she says. Clay takes her hand and leads her away, her little fingers clenched together beneath the tight grip of his cold clammy hand.* The image bombarded my brain. I sucked in air, making a sound you might make if someone stuck a knife in your gut.

"I thought I had kept you safe from that bastard," I said in a high squeaky voice. I slouched forward, clinging to the arms of the chair. Angel had gone blurry on me. I couldn't see her face. Not that it mattered. I wouldn't have been able to look her straight in the eye anyway. I felt the room spinning all around me, the floor pressing up against my feet until my chin rested on my knees. I heard a buzz humming noise like a thousand swarming bumblebees buzzing round and round inside my head.

My anger began to boil in the back of my mind. Molten rage began to glow, boiled over and spilled into my veins. I sprung from my chair and stumbled across the room like a wounded Grizzly. I wanted to find Clay and rip him to pieces. "That does it," I said. "Where is that sonofabitch?"

"I have his mother's phone number. She's still in Idaho. Maybe she knows where he is," Angel said, reaching for her address book. In the address book was a scrap of paper that had been folded, unfolded and refolded many times. On it was written "Clay's mother" and a phone number. She handed it to me. "I was afraid to call," she said.

"I'm not. I'm not some scared little girl now," I said. "I'm not afraid of Clay Stout."

She handed me the phone. "You call."

I dialed the number. A woman answered. "May I speak to Clayton Stout?" I asked.

"This is his mother. He isn't here right now. He'll be back in a few hours."

I hung up.

"Are you going to call back?"

I shook my head. "No," I said, "I don't want him to know we know where he is. I'm going to kill him." I remembered the knife in the trunk Mama had brought with her to my house. It was the knife Grandpa had made. He had cut the twelve-inch blade from a piece of steel, hammered it and shaped it so that the point curved off to one side, then sharpened the edge until it was razor-sharp.

My heart beat slow and steady. I was calm. I sat with the knife on my lap. I had decided to use the knife. I knew how I would do it. I had dreamed of doing it. I would look him straight in the eye. "Remember me?" I would ask. "Remember Angel Puss?"

And then I would slit his throat.

Angel and I talked into the night, saying words that we had never spoken before. Nodding. Understanding. We took turns saying the unspeakable.

"I tried to protect you," I said. "I thought I did."

She said, "Remember Castle Rock? Remember me asking you if you were the other one? You used to turn into somebody else, and you couldn't remember things. I tried to help you so you would know what to do."

"If it wasn't for you, I would have been completely lost. You probably kept me from ending up in a padded cell."

We stayed up all night talking. Remembering. One of us said, "We were so little." The other said, "Poor little things." We cried for the two little girls that had been disrespected. Violated. At some point we cried for ourselves and all those lost years, as we made poor choices in our struggle to find happiness. We didn't know any better. Our growth had been stunted. Our whole lives had been shaped by events over which we had no control.

We cried and cried and cried.

As the sun came up, flooding the room with light, Angel put on a pot of coffee. "Are you really going to kill him?" she asked.

Oddly, after all those years of plotting how I would kill him once I found him, now that I knew where he was, I no longer needed to kill him. "I'm not going to bother with him" I said. "He's not worth one more minute of our life. Let's be done with him."

I took a sip of coffee. "You know, bad men flourish in the darkness, and now that we have told his secrets, he has no power. He is seen for what he is."

I picked up the phone, took Angel's yellowed paper from my pocket and dialed. Clay's mother answered. "Hello," I said. This is Lucinda, one of the little girls your son violated. Your son molests and rapes little girls. Even babies. I think you know that. But in case you didn't already know, you know now."

I hung up.

Then I called the sheriff in Port Gamble. "This is going to be the strangest call you've ever gotten," I said. "Forty years ago, Clayton Stout raped me. I was seven years old. He molested my little sister. He raped a baby in a car in front of a department store in 1946. It was Bremerton. Maybe Port Gamble. There must be some detective who worked the case, and parents, saddened because the case was never solved."

I took a deep breath and continued, "Clay lives with his mother in a two-story farmhouse somewhere in Idaho. This is the phone number. If you have unsolved cases involving little girls, I'd look at him."

The sheriff thanked me and asked for my telephone number. I gave it to him.

A few days later, the sheriff called. "We located him. His full name is Lawton Clayton Stout. We located court records from your original case against him. Of course, nothing can be done with that case, as the stature of limitations has run out. But we now consider him a suspect in other more recent cases. Do you want to be notified of the outcomes?"

"No," I said. "I'm done with that sonofabitch."

That night, I woke from a sound sleep. If was half past midnight. It was dark. It was quiet. The television was not on. I jumped up and peeked in Angel's bedroom.

Angel was sleeping peacefully.

33

As the years passed by, my life seemed somewhat ordinary. No one knew how unordinary it was. Not even me. And then, I became aware of odd things happening: In my closet was an outfit I had never seen before. A designer suit, it was nicer than anything I had ever owned. I tried it on. To my surprise, it fit perfectly. Even the hem was right where I liked it- just below the knee. It was as if it had been tailored just for me. One day, I found a handful of loose pills in my desk drawer that I thought I had taken as prescribed.

Once, I got in my car, headed to work, and found myself driving across the George Washington bridge in New York City. I was one hundred sixty-eight miles from my office. I had been driving for three hours and had no recollection of having done so.

Suddenly, the sky turned dark, and it began to rain. At first, just a few drops, then the rain came faster, falling in sheets, cascading down the windshield. I remembered other rain:

...Something terrible has happened but I don't know what. Windshield wipers work furiously, yet useless against the relentless rain... *Wow, this rain is bad. I need to turn on the windshield wipers. At least they'll help a little.* But I couldn't figure out how to turn them on. I pulled into a truck stop and tried to figure out how to make the wipers work.

I could not remember.

The wind was blowing on the river below, making the water choppy. I thought I heard somebody say, *Take the ferry. It'll be quicker...*

...I woke to a loud pounding on my car window. "Lady, are you okay?" the truck driver wanted to know.

"I'm fine. Just resting up before I drive across the bridge."

"Better wait until the wind dies down. the bridge sways in rough weather. Me, I'm going to wait until it's over."

Two hours later, the rain stopped, and the wind calmed down. But now I couldn't remember how to start the car.

I did not know how to drive.

I went to work one day and didn't know any of my co-workers. I didn't know how to turn on my computer. And I could hear a little girl crying. I looked out in the hall, in the conference room and in the ladies room but I couldn't find her.

I had lunch that day with a client who happened to be a psychologist. During lunch, I heard the child again. "Listen," I said. "I hear a little girl crying."

"I don't hear anything."

"Seems like everywhere I go, I hear a little girl crying."

She looked at me with an odd expression on her face, like she had just swallowed a lemon. "I think," she said, "I think that you are hearing your own inner child. Did you have a traumatic childhood?"

I squirmed. I was uncomfortable sharing person information with a client. I nodded.

"Here," she said, handing me a business card of a colleague. "Talk to him. I think he can help you find the sad little girl that lives inside your head."

"Thanks." I did not know what else to say.

Well, that was weird, I thought. *Things are not quite right. But I don't need a shrink.*

———————— ◆ ◆ ————————

My memory was becoming worse. It was interfering with my life. My husband took to whispering clues when we ran into someone we knew. "The woman in the blue dress, headed this way. It's Sandra. she's the librarian." "The guy bringing you a drink, he's John. He's a good friend. This is his house."

I missed my children's school functions. To them, it must have seemed as if I didn't care. The memory problems had taken over my life.

In addition to having to deal with memory gaps, and chunks of lost time, I was becoming more and more unhappy in my marriage. In an effort to save marriage number five, I called the psychologist my client friend had recommended. He agreed to see us the following week.

Young Doctor Elan reminded me of photos I had seen of Sigmund Freud when he was young. His beard wasn't too long, and it was neatly trimmed. I liked his thoughtful eyes. I was amused by the half smile on his face, as if he knew that this might not be a time to be cheerful.

The office was elegant, yet comfortable. Richly paneled walls. Persian rug. A Pegasus sculpture on the large traditional desk. *Hmmmm,*

I thought, *either he comes from money, or he is successful in his own right*. And I dared to hope that he was good at what he did, whatever it was that psychologists do.

"Have a seat," he said. We sat in tufted leather chairs facing him. I was pleased that he did not sit behind the large mahogany desk in front of the window.

The session went better than I expected. He asked us what problems we were having, and what we hoped to accomplish. Things like that. As we talked, Doctor Elan held a black leather notebook in his left hand. In his right hand was a gold pen, with which he wrote every now and then.

We met with Doctor Elan half a dozen times, my husband and me. Then one day Doctor Elan asked me to come in alone.

I left work early on the day of my appointment with Doctor Elan. I wanted to change my clothes. I had no idea why. I was feeling giddy. I had no idea why I was excited about the session with Doctor Elan. I felt like I was involved in some sort of surprise.

It had begun to snow. I drove home with snowflakes splattering on the windshield, making patterns like tiny, crocheted doilies. The streets were covered in white, making everything clean.

I changed into my best suit, a winter white Dior with a white silk blouse. I slipped into my Blackgama mink and pulled on Italian leather gloves. I knew the gloves would not keep my hands warm, but I liked how they looked.

I felt a huge smile on my face that I hadn't put there. And when Doctor Elan opened the door, I put out my hand and said, "So nice to finally meet you." I thought, *How silly. I've been here before*.

"Nice to meet you," Doctor Elan said. "Come in."

I sat on the edge of the chair, staring at the wall of leather-bound books.

"How are things going?" he asked.

"Well, to be honest. I don't see any purpose in continuing marriage counseling," I said. "We aren't getting along. And I think my husband is gay. He spends way too much time with one guy in particular. And sometimes he points out what a nice build some guy has."

"I think you are right," he said.

That settled, I lunged into the real reason he had asked me to meet with him alone. "So, what do you know about me?" I asked.

"I think you have multiple personalities. I think that they switch often, and that's why you have gaps in memory."

When he said that, I knew it was so. "So, I *am* crazy," I said.

"No. Dissociative Identity Disorder is a device highly intelligent children use in order to avoid having to deal with trauma."

"Highly intelligent. I like that," I said flippantly." I put a smile on my face. Not a real one. Fake.

Now that I knew the truth, what was I to do?

34

I continued to see Doctor Elan alone. At his suggestion, I took a leave of absence from my job while I sorted things out. In the past, I had created other selves to suit the circumstances. This time would be different.

This time I would be true to myself.

During the sessions with Doctor Elan, he would ask about my past. "What happened with your marriages?" he asked. "Why didn't they work?"

"Well, the first one cheated on me, and he beat me up."

"Go on."

"J.D. had broken my nose when we lived in California. Then he sailed to India. I got a job with Vic Tanny Gyms and was promoted to manager. I was doing well. I moved into a luxury townhouse with a pool and furnished it with Danish modern. When J.D. came home and told me he wouldn't be going out on ship anymore because they took away his union card, I didn't care.

"Now J.D. followed me around like a lovesick hound dog. He used his last paycheck to buy me an ivory cashmere coat, soft as dandelion down. "You look good," he said. "They call you 'The Body' at Vic Tanny's. Ain't that bitchin'?"

"What did you think when you learned they called you 'The Body'?"

"I knew about the one he was talking about. It wasn't *me*. Sometimes she would just shove me aside and take over. I envied her. *The Body* oozed confidence. She was so comfortable with her sexuality that it made me blush. She wasn't crude or crass- just comfortable with her body. I, on the other hand, walked with my shoulders forward so as not to bring attention to my breasts. I was uncomfortable around men. I had no idea why."

"So, you were aware of another side of your personality?"

"I did know something was different. I used to run to the mirror as soon as I woke up. I could tell by the eyes if I would be feeling different. And sometimes I would act different, and I wouldn't be able to stop, like I might burst into tears at work if I forgot how to do something, or prance around in a bikini. Stuff like that."

"Anything else?"

"Well, less than two weeks after J.D. gave me the coat, it turned up missing. I mentioned it at work and someone, I don't remember who, told me that J.D. had given it to Audrey. So I asked J.D. about it, and he said it was at the cleaners. I called him a liar, and he came at me, his fist doubled. And I turned into somebody else. I said, 'Who do you think you're talking to?' I had a long, sharp knife in my hand. I heard a voice coming from my mouth say, 'You take one step towards me and I'll kill you.' We stood glowering at one another for several minutes, not saying a word. J.D. decided I meant it and put down his fists."

"What did you do?"

"I lowered the knife and told him I knew he'd been cheating the whole time. He admitted it and reeled off names of women I had suspected and some I hadn't, then said, 'And your mother.'"

"Your own mother? He said he'd been with her?"

I knew it was true. As soon as he said it, I remembered Mama sneaking up the basement stairs in the house in Molalla. I remembered

Mama and J.D. leaving me alone on my wedding day. I waved the knife in the air. J.D. took off running, and, next thing I knew, I was chasing after him. Another me followed along, flying, watching the whole thing, amused to see a big tough guy running from a hundred twenty-two-pound woman. Funny, but not such a good idea. I quit flying and hid in the black space inside myself."

"Black space?"

"I guess sometimes I black out. That's when I have trouble remembering things. I call it the black space."

Doctor Elan scribbled in the notebook. "What happened after that?"

"I heard sirens off in the distance. People gathered round to stare. I was holding a knife, wondering, *How I get in this kettle of worms? And where did I get the knife?*"

"What did you do with the knife?"

"A man came out of the barbershop and gently took the knife. 'You go home now,' he said, 'No kill husband.' I remember it was very hot. The air was still. Heavy. The sky was dingy gray and a red sun had appeared low in the sky. I remember standing perfectly still, watching it drop lower and lower until it disappeared behind some trees."

Doctor Elan leaned forward. "How long did you stand there?"

"Until it was dark, then I headed home. There was a telephone booth on the corner. I stepped inside. Someone at work had given me Audrey's number. I dialed it. 'Lo', she said. Her voice was very sexy."

"That must have been difficult for you. What did you say?"

"Hello, Audrey. This is J.D.'s wife. Since you and J.D. are such good friends, why don't we go out to lunch and get to know each other?"

"There was a long pause before she answered. 'I didn't know he was married.' Her surprise seemed genuine."

Doctor Elan stroked his beard, and then wrote something in his notebook.

I continued. I said, 'Oh, really? Well, then you probably don't know that the coat he gave you is mine. You don't mind if I come and pick it up, do you?' I took back the coat and a little of my self-respect"

"That must have made you feel better."

I shrugged. "Things changed after that. Audrey wouldn't have anything to do with J.D. anymore. J.D. did his best to stay on the good side of me. I didn't throw him out. I had married for better or worse but if he reached for me in the dark I said, 'Don't touch me.' When J.D. moved back to Portland, I gave up my good job and went with him. It never occurred to me that I had a choice. It was 1958. I was only eighteen and had two little boys. Women were supposed to go wherever their husbands went, and I had learned at an early age that women do what men want."

"That's all the time we have for today. We can pick up where we left off next week."

35

~~~~~~~~~~~~~~~~

A t the next session, Doctor E. asked, "Did you eventually divorce J.D.?

"Not until later. I got a job managing a gym and he found a job, too. But within a few weeks he was fired. He hit the bars. 'That boy can't keep a job,' they said. 'Never will. Wonder where he got that chip on his shoulder.' I thought it was my fault for calling him a bastard, so when he wanted me to move back to Portland with him, I went."

"I was sound asleep when J.D. came home and pounded on the door. Groggy, I didn't answer the door fast enough to suit him. He stumbled towards me, his eyes vacant, staring without seeing. "Didn't you hear me knocking, Bitch?" I smelled whiskey on his breath. I turned away. His fist slammed into the right side of my head. There was an ear-splitting ringing in my ear. He shoved me down on the bed, pounding his fist into my face. I closed my eyes, grateful for a safe dark place to hide."

Doctor E. shook his head.

I continued, "Next day at work they whispered, pointed and stared. 'Oh my God, would you look at that,' they said, 'What happened to her?'

"I lied to explain my tri-colored face. 'I slipped in the shower and fell,' I said. Truthfully, I couldn't remember what had happened.

"Unsure of what exactly I did at work, I stood at the door and asked everyone the same question. 'Would you like a tour of the gym?' I asked a plump gray-haired woman as she walked in the door.

"She looked at me strangely. 'You know me. I come here every day.' I looked at her carefully. I would have sworn I had never seen her before in my life. She put her arm around me. 'What's your name?' she asked gently.

"I couldn't remember. 'It's right on the tip of my tongue,' I said, and then told her my maiden name. She shook her head like she knew my name better than I did. 'Wait,' I said, as I struggled to remember. 'I'll remember my name in a minute.' The woman I couldn't remember was pushing me towards the door. 'I'm a nurse,' she said. 'I'm taking you to the hospital. You have a concussion.' I told her I was alright."

"Did she believe you?"

"No. She took me by the hand and led me to a mirror. 'Look at yourself.' The face in the mirror was ashen. The right ear swollen. Purple. One eye blue-purple-black. It was the eyes that concerned her. Black, like two dark holes in a khaki face. I was fascinated with the face, that multi-colored blotch. I knew the face as well as I knew my own name. I recognized the eyes. They were the eyes of a child I had once been."

"So, on some level, you knew there was another personality?"

"I did know that the eyes that looked back at me in the mirror were sometimes different."

Talking about multiple personalities made me more uncomfortable than talking about getting beat up, so I went on the story. "I could hear humming, buzzing, a loud buzz-humming sound as if a bee had gotten inside my head and couldn't get out. 'The noise is in your head,' the doctor said, 'Your eardrum is broken.' He was shining a flashlight in my eyes. 'What year is it?'

" '1947,' I said. The doctor gave me a look I couldn't figure. I glanced at the calendar on the wall. It said December 1958."

" 'Where do you live?' The doctor asked. And I said, 'By the lighthouse.' Then he asked, 'What's your address?' And I said, 'Go to the fire hydrant, then count one, two, three, four, five. That's my house,' I was admitted to the hospital. The doctor was concerned about my memory loss."

"How long were you hospitalized?"

"I was in the hospital six days. When I was discharged, the nurse told J.D. 'Your wife needs to go to bed and stay there. Don't let her walk around. If she gets a blood clot in her brain it could kill her. Have her downstairs at three o'clock.' At 2:50 a nurse took me to the lobby to wait. At 3:10 a Yellow Cab pulled up. 'J.D. sent me,' the driver said. I climbed in wondering, *Why didn't J.D. come himself?* The cab stopped in front of the pharmacy, six, eight blocks from the apartment. J.D. was waiting for me. He paid the driver and sent him away. 'Let's go,' J.D. said, grabbing my arm. I said, 'I'm not supposed to be walking.' And J.D. shrugged and said, 'So?'"

Doctor E. was leaning towards me, his notebook forgotten. I continued, "I stood still, not breathing, my head down. I stared at a crack in the sidewalk. *The Sadness* rose up out of the crack and jumped on my shoulders. *'J.D. wants you dead!'* it whispered hoarsely. I pulled away from J.D., went inside the pharmacy, called Mama and asked her to come get me."

Doctor E. nodded, like I had done right.

"It all happened in slow motion, like in a dream," I explained. "I had been at Mama's two weeks when I opened the door and stood face to face with J.D. He had a suitcase in his hand. 'Go away,' I said. Mama pushed me aside and told him he could stay the night. That evening, I noticed that J.D had been upstairs a long time. I took off my shoes and tiptoed up the stairs to see what J.D. was doing. He was lying across my bed on his stomach, peeping down the floor register. I snuck up behind him and peeked over his shoulder into the bathroom below. Mama was posed with one foot on the edge of the tub, her butt stuck out, soaping her body slowly like she was the star in a porn film. I tapped J.D. on the shoulder. 'Get out,' I said in a slow, quiet voice I hardly recognized. I turned, walked down the stairs, and waited for J.D. to pack and leave."

"Did he leave?"

"No. J.D. sauntered downstairs and sat down in front of the TV. 'I want you out!' I said."

Remembering what came next, I started to giggle. "What's funny?" Doctor Elan asked.

"Well, J.D. said, 'So? Who cares what you want?' His eyes were icy, his lips pressed tightly into a thin, hard line. '*I* care,' I said. 'Get out!' J.D. didn't budge. 'Get outta my face,' he said.

"Oh my, were you afraid?"

"No. J.D. made me so angry, sitting there looking smug, I turned into somebody else. I was thinking about knocking that smug smile off his face. I was thinking about doubling up my fist and knocking his teeth out. 'Who do you think you're talking to?' I heard myself say. 'Nobody talks to *me* like that.'"

Doctor E. picked up his notebook and wrote something in it.

"'What you gonna do about it?' J.D. wanted to know. He had no idea who he was talking to. I picked up the rocking chair that Grandpa had made for Danny and whacked him upside the head. Hard. 'Now, get out,' I said quietly. 'And don't ever come back or I'll tell Grandpa how I got this broken ear drum.' J.D. looked at me in disbelief. Without a word he got up and walked out the door. That's the last I ever saw of him."

Doctor E. was doing his best to remain professional but I'm pretty sure he smiled.

66 Have you thought about why you picked the men you married?" Doctor Elan asked.

I studied the medallion in the center of the Persian carpet. It was two shades of red, outlined in gold. "I like your carpet," I said. Doctor Elan was staring at me, waiting for an answer. "This is a nice office," I said.

Doctor Elan said nothing. He expected an answer.

"Well, for one thing. I didn't pick them. They picked me. Things were different back then. I did what they wanted. I didn't really think about what I wanted."

"I see, he said, as he guided his pen across the page of his always present notebook. "What about the other marriages? What went wrong there?"

"The next marriage was just as bad as the first. Only God knows what I saw in Bob. He was good in bed. I'll give him that. But that's never enough. No matter how long the night. No matter how hot the blood pulsing through your veins. No matter how eagerly you arch your back in anticipation of the next thrust. No matter, Morning always comes. And, in the light of day, gods become swine, and many a man is not so tall, after all."

Doctor Elan wrote in his notebook. "That's pretty astute," he said. And this time, he grinned.

"Bob wanted to elope. He said he would take care of everything. The following Saturday I waited with Bob for the city bus that would take us to the bus station. It was a brisk and windy day in March. I was chilled to the bone. The wind whipped my hair across my face. I reached up to brush it away, my hand came away wet with tears. It was my wedding day. I had expected something else. In my fantasy, Bob arrived with a large package under one arm. In it a beautiful, embroidered wedding gown. It would be icy blue or maybe yellow, and there would be rosebuds and lilies tied with white satin. Instead, Bob arrived with a newspaper under one arm. Now I followed him onto the city bus, and sat, staring out the window, while he read the news. We didn't talk.

"We climbed aboard a Greyhound that would take us across the state line. I thought maybe Bob wanted to go someplace special for dinner or maybe stay overnight in a nice hotel. Instead, we said our I do's in a hot, dusty desert town, ate hot dogs at the bus station, got on the bus and headed home."

"Not the wedding you envisioned. How did that affect you?"

"I could not, for the life of me, figure out why Bob wanted to get married in Arizona."

"Hmmm," Doctor Elan said.

"My third baby, a girl, was born while Bob sat in the hospital cafeteria reading the newspaper. Three weeks later, he packed up and left. I was only 22 and had 3 children. Unable to pay the rent without help, I took the kids and, leaving everything behind, trudged down the street, without a thought to where I would go. Later, I tried to retrace my steps but couldn't remember where I lived.

"Eventually, Bob found me and brought me back. Then, one evening, I set the table with a white tablecloth and good china, like every night. As I served dinner, I asked Bob if he could babysit because I had an exam, and the babysitter couldn't do it. I had three kids, worked full time at the telephone company, and attended college nights. I needed some help."

"That is a lot for one woman. How old were you then?"

"Twenty-two."

Doctor Elan shook his head.

"When I asked Bob to babysit, he jumped up and pounded his fist on the table. 'Don't tell me what to do!' he yelled, grabbing the tablecloth, and pulling it off the table, knocking pork chops into Danny's lap. Mashed potatoes splattered Stevie. Glasses crashed to the floor. Aurora's eyes opened wide. She let out a howl. 'Don't tell me what to do!' Bob screamed, as he ran out the door.

"I ran after him, catching up with him in the alley. I reached out and touched his arm. 'What's the matter? What''s wrong?'

" 'Don't *ever* tell me what to do again!' His fist plowed into my nose. The child within me took the beating. 'You're killing me,' she whimpered, her mouth full of blood.

" 'Then die,' Bob said coldly, showing no mercy. Fists hammered the child's head. Face. Stomach. She fell to the ground and curled up in a ball, trying to protect herself. Bob kicked her, his hard shoe battering her back.

"Cars slowed. People gawked. A skinny freckled red-haired boy, riding by on his bicycle, stopped. Tears streamed down his cheeks. 'Please, Mister, please don't hit her anymore.'

"Bob delivered one last kick, then turned and walked away. The skinny kid helped me up. 'What can I do? How can I help?'

The child sobbed, 'I want my mama.' She closed her eyes and disappeared...

..." 'Tell my baby-sitter to put the kids in the bedroom and call the police,' I said to the freckled face boy. I pointed to the apartment building. The boy took off running, leaving his bicycle lying on the ground next to me. 'Apartment number two,' I yelled after him.

"The boy did as he was told, then returned to help the child limp home.

"Police took the child to the hospital in a cruiser, siren screaming, blue lights flashing. A policewoman photographed her in only her panties, noting numerous bruises. Police report: Domestic violence. Assault and Battery. Doctor's report: Tooth knocked out. Four chipped teeth. Several loose teeth. Broken nose. Ruptured eardrum. Severe damage to left cornea. Bruises. Contusions. Possible broken jaw.

"Hours later we returned to the apartment, two plainclothes cops and I. 'We'll wait here,' one said. 'He'll be back.'

" 'I don't think so,' I said, 'not after what he's done.'

" 'He'll be back. They always come back.'

"The child sat motionless- a pale lump, hunkered down in the corner of the sofa, her eyes grown large and luminous, like a frightened little mouse. She sat so still it prompted the policeman to ask if she was all right. She nodded.

"He whispered to his partner, 'She's such a little thing, so innocent. Childlike.'

"When the telephone rang, they knew it was him. The cop picked up the phone and handed it to me. 'I'm standing here in the phone booth and I'm cold,' Bob said.

" 'What?' I said.

" 'I'm standing here in the phone booth and I'm cold.'

" The policeman whispered, 'Tell him to come home.'

" 'Come home,' I said into the phone.

" 'You're under arrest,' the policeman said when Bob walked in the door. As Bob was handcuffed and led out of the apartment, he turned and looked at me as if *I* had betrayed *him*.

"I kicked off my shoes and crawled into bed fully dressed. I was not sleep. I was not awake. Suspended in a gray world, I felt nothing. I stumbled to the bath and flipped on the light. I saw a reflection, an unreal vision, in my mirror. Purple lumpy face. Broad blue-black nose.

The Sadness squeezed my heart harder and harder, until a bloodstained tear formed in the corner of a swollen, blood-streaked eye. The red tear crept slowly down a misshapen cheek, followed by another and another."

Doctor Elan turned away. I think I saw him wipe away a tear.

I looked down, staring at the medallion in the center of the Persian carpet that spanned the room, then continued. "At court, the bailiff led the prisoners into the courtroom, chained together at the ankles. Bob hadn't shaved. He was rumpled. Subdued. Handcuffed, same as the others. He looked pitiful. I thought back to Bob's odd phone call. 'I'm standing here in the phone booth and I'm cold,' he had said. I decided Bob needed counseling, not jail. I asked him if he'd go for counseling if I dropped the charges. He promised. He promised but he didn't go. He never once told me he was sorry. He wouldn't look at me; otherwise, he acted like nothing happened. And that night Bob reached for me in bed. 'I don't feel like it,' I said."

" 'Well, then, you're no good to me.'

Doctor Elan opened his mouth to say something, then just motioned for me to continue.

" 'Next morning the sun rose, as if it was an ordinary day, and we set out on our customary Saturday morning walk to the park. Birds sang, oblivious to The Sadness, which was much stronger now. Heavier. Meaner. The Sadness sat, perched on my shoulders like a vulture. With each step The Sadness bit off a piece of me, chomping down hard, chewing me up, spitting me out, leaving a trail of bloody pieces behind.

"I pushed the stroller in slow motion, dragging my feet towards the park, my face swollen and discolored. I wore dark glasses, as the doctor ordered, to protect my damaged cornea. A man and woman walked towards us. The woman stared. The man looked away. Bob glared at me. 'Cover your face,' he said.

"And I turned into somebody else...

"*The Protector* sent the boys on ahead. Danny was five. Stevie four. They marched on, pushing their baby sister in the stroller, their sturdy little legs propelling them towards the park. When they were out of earshot, I heard a quiet quiet voice say, 'I'm not hiding *my* face.

You did this to me. You should hide *your* face.' I looked at my watch. 'It's two o'clock," I said, 'I'm coming home at five. You'd better be gone. Don't ever come back. Don't ever call. If you're not gone when I get back, you'll never be able to close your eyes again because I'll kill you while you sleep. Nobody hits *me*.'

"Bob looked at me dumb founded, then turned and walked away. He called me at work, but I wouldn't take the calls. I never saw Bob again."

I could tell Doctor Elan was shocked, but he would never have said so. Instead, he continued as if getting battered and bruised was something he heard every day. Maybe it was.

"What about the others?" Doctor Elan was holding his pen in his hand, ready to write whatever it was he wrote in his notebook.

"The next three didn't beat me. But they didn't treat me right. They lied. They cheated. They didn't pull their weight financially. I feel sometimes like I didn't marry five different men; it's more like I married the same man five different times. They were all the same. I expected honor. Loyalty. Respect. Love. When I didn't get it, I left. It was the right thing to do."

Doctor Elan looked at this watch. "That's all the time we have for today," he said. "Next week, I'd like to know a little about your mother."

37

I had decided to tell Doctor Elan about Mama's betrayal- the worst one. I told him all about the dog beast that had flashed into my mind, and how eventually I realized Mama had gone back to Clay after what happened. I explained that I knew that because Clay was in the car when we got my dog, Jack, and drove to Trinidad, Colorado, a whole year after she knew what he had done.

I told the story in a straightforward manner and did not offer any insight to how I fell about it. Doctor Elan understood without being told. He stroked his neatly clipped beard and peered at me with eyes that saw way more than I was ready for him to see.

He changed the subject. "Did you move a lot?" he asked.

"I have moved over four dozen times. If you said you'd give me a million dollars for each address I can remember *if* I could remember them all, I would only be able to tell you one address: 412 West A Street. My grandpa's house in Grants Pass, Oregon."

He was staring at me in disbelief.

"Yeah, I moved a lot. I went to eight schools before high school, six high schools, four Junior colleges and five colleges. I changed names a lot, too. Every time Mama got married she changed our last name. Five times that I can remember. Then I got married five times, if you want to count the one that was married to somebody else when he married me."

"You were married to a bigamist? When was that?"

"Oh, that's why Bob wanted to elope. That's why he wanted to get married in Arizona. He was already had a wife in California."

I fiddled with my handbag, embarrassed at how foolish and naive I had been. "So that's a dozen names," I said. "No wonder I'm screwed up. I've had so many names that I don't even know who I am."

Doctor Elan moved his pen over his notebook. Then he looked me in the eye. "And then there are your multiple personalities. Do you know who they are?"

When he said that, I changed into somebody else. An equal. The one who advised psychologists, attorneys and even a judge on financial matters. I was tired of the psychobabble. I stood to leave. "They aren't *people*, I said. "They are just misplaced memories."

"Oh, so you know that." he sounded pleased. "Please sit down. We still have time."

I sat reluctantly. "Well, I know there is a child, maybe more— "

He looked at me as if he expected clarification.

"The first one, the one who suffered, that part of me just up and disappeared. That was *The Child*." Before I could continue, I was interrupted by the sound of a little girl sobbing. She was very near. I turned and looked behind me. There was no one there. "Do you hear that?" I asked. "Do you hear a child crying?"

"No, I can't hear her. Only you can hear her. She's your inner child. She wants you to acknowledge her. Can you see her?"

I was thinking, *Is he the crazy one?* "No," I said annoyed. "I can't *see* her." *This is gobbledygook.* I sighed and shook my head.

Doctor Elan was looking right at me. Watching me. "Try to see the little girl who's crying," he said. "A terrible thing has happened to her. That's why she's hiding. Close your eyes. Try to see her."

I closed my eyes, expecting to escape the ridiculous shrink talk. But in the dark place inside my head, I found no solace. I could not hide. And I was not alone. The sadness had tiptoed into my head, parading my many selves before me. Now I understood. Others lived inside my head. And now I saw them: *The Child* crouched down in the far corner of my mind, sobbing pitifully, the child I heard so many times, crying in the darkness, the part of myself that had suffered. Disappeared. I needed to get her back. I reached inside myself and embraced the child within.

I cried real tears.

"Do you see the others?" Doctor Elan asked. And now I saw another little girl. *The Other Child* continues to play, oblivious to what is happening to *The Child.* She knows nothing of what Clay has done. When *The Child* disappeared, I had turned into somebody else, *The Other Child*, who knew nothing about the bad stuff that had happened. She had no painful memories. She had aged along with me.

My third inner child was seven years old. She stands in the kitchen brandishing a sharp knife, making stabbing motions in the air. She is *The Protector*. She wants to kill Clayton Stout. Even when I was grown, when my memories surfaces, and when I remembered what he had done, and how he had broken the child within me, *The Protector*, who had not aged, had dreamed up a thousand ways to kill him.

As I discovered my many selves, I drew sketches of them, so that I could distinguish one from the other. *The Child, The Other Child. The Protector. The Body. The Artist. The Student. The Stockbroker.* I could see them clearly now. I gulped in air. I let out my breath. It made a sound like a mighty sorrowful wind.

38

Difficult as it was, I knew I needed to confront the past before I could change the future. Now that repressed memories had surfaced, now that I was aware of my multiple identities, I accepted my multi-faceted self. And, as time went by, they began to cooperate, and no longer popped out at inappropriate times. Eventually, we merged. I became the *Stockbroker*, the strongest, most confident one. I made it possible for the others to make themselves known. I allowed them to stay.

The Child healed once her story was told. I now know all that happened. *The Body* was health conscious and comfortable with her body. She kept me from hating all men, which sometimes happens to wounded women. *The Student* gave me an education, which, in spite of interruptions, taught me so much that I could not have known otherwise. I could not have become *The Stockbroker* without the help of *The Student*. *The Protector* matured. She no longer grabs knives and waves them in the air. She was, after all, only seven years old. She was scared. All talk. She would never have killed anybody. It was an empty threat. That protective part of me will not let anybody take advantage of me. I am one of the nicest little ole ladies you'll ever meet, but if you disrespect me, I can be a sonofabitch. Kick in my door, and I will sue you. Cheat on me, and I will divorce you. Betray me, and I will no longer be your friend.

Much has happened. And now I remember it all. For me, time moved not as it ought, but flickered in and out of my mind. What was yesterday, and what is today was all jumbled together, and when I remembered what happened, it happened not in the past, but became a present terror.

Sometimes, the sadness overwhelms me and I burst into tears, filled with regret. I should have done this. I shouldn't have done that. I am sometimes reluctant to make decisions because I made so many bad ones in the past. Even though I am far from perfect, I accept who I am. I think I turned out pretty good considering what I went through.

I have many memories of good times and wonderful, loving people in my life. As the years go by, the good far outweighs the bad.

I am no longer splintered.

THE END

Dear Reader,

Please take a moment and leave a book review. If you purchased from Amazon or Barnes and Noble, leave your review on their site. To do a review on Amazon, go to your order and select this book. At the bottom, it will ask you to review the product. Please add your review there. Barnes and Noble is the same.

If you purchased from Bronze Goose Books, or through an independent bookstore anywhere in the world, please post a review on Goodreads. Go to www.goodreads.com. At the top of the page, type in the title of the book, then complete your review.

Thank you for your support.

Yours Truly,

LuWanda M Cheney

ABOUT THE AUTHOR

LuWanda M. Cheney is an American author. She is an imaginative storyteller now living in New England. She was born in Dayton, Washington on March 8, 1940. As a child, Cheney loved to read and write short stories. A high school dropout, she became the first in her family to attend college. A single parent, she attended several colleges while working full time before graduating from Long Beach City College in 1967. At age 38 she graduated from Worcester State College where she won 1st place in the Lenora Knight short story contest and received a Fellowship to UMass MFA Program. She left the program after a year, then attended law school for a year. Despite frequent moves, marriages and divorces, Cheney became one of few successful female stockbrokers in 1977. In her spare time, she wrote newspaper columns, ad copy, novels, and short stories.

Soon to be released:

On Her Feet is a true story written by Ashley and her mother. When thirteen-year-old Ashley jumps off the roof, thinking it will be fun, she suffers a permanent spinal cord injury. Her brilliant doctors tell her she will never walk again, but her mother tells her she can. Who will she choose to trust?

Secrets is a novel about Webster, an eleven-year-old girl, who spies on the townspeople in the small town of Rock Point. She uncovers shocking secrets but vows never to tell. Will she break her vow of secrecy and tell what she knows, in order to help find Ruby, her sixteen-year-old friend who has mysteriously disappeared?

CPSIA information can be obtained
at www.ICGtesting.com
Printed in the USA
BVHW091310090422
633358BV00004B/19